CHECK UP FROM YOUR NECK UP

CHECK UP FROM YOUR NECK UP

52 WEEKLY MANTRAS
TO LIVE YOUR BEST LIFE

MARIE HELTON TRIPLETT

ISBN: 978-1-7328116-3-8

To my stud muffin husband, Mike, thank you for believing in me even when I didn't believe in myself. To my incredible sons, Jalen, Alex, and Christian, there is nothing in the world more important to me than you. Thank you for all your love and support. I could not have done this without you giving me strength, and I hope I make you proud! Love you to the moon and back.

I want to thank my extended family for loving me through the worst of times and cheering for me during the happiest times. Grandma, thank you for teaching me that running away from my problems isn't the answer and how to be a boss in the kitchen. Aunt Michelle A.K.A. Nina, I'm eternally grateful for you taking me in and loving me as one of your own, I know I was the most difficult, but I also know I am your favorite. :)

I'd like to thank the people that helped this dream become a reality. My Editor Amy Li and Designer, Jennifer Toomey, you ladies, helped me shine this bad boy up into something I am proud of. My Photographer, Stephanie Gonzales, your ability to take my awkward ass and turn it into the cover art is pure magic.

Finally, a big shout out to my brother Tarak Uday and Awaken Within Media; I know I am the big sister, but without you guiding me through this process, there is no way in Hell, I would have finished it on time.

INTRODUCTION

Raise your hand if you're sick and tired of being sick and tired. Do you feel a deep pull in your gut to make changes but have no idea where to start? This is an incredibly frustrating place to be. Trust me when I say I feel your pain. Truly, madly, deeply, I do. I was in this very position a few years ago. I was lost. I wanted more but didn't know how to begin. My identity was wrapped up in the hats I wore— mom, wife, and employee but I just kept asking myself, "where is Marie?" I was dying a slow death and knew I needed to make changes.

After some significant time in self-discovery, I realized that the outside world is a mirror image of the inside world. You can't create a better external life until you fix the brokenness in your mind. So, I've spent the last few years working on me. Yes, *years* working on me. I know that may seem dramatic, but I had a lifetime of lousy programming to work through—feelings of worthlessness, and a litany of insecurities. I had held on to so much of my pain from past that it held me back from stepping forward. My past paralyzed me, and it festered in the form of social anxiety, introverted tendencies, and extreme fear.

During this journey, I have had many "ah-ha" moments that I have compiled into what is now this book. I've found my voice, learned that being brave won't kill me (even though it feels like it will), and realized there is a whole new fantastic world on the other side of my issues that was worth every tear cried along the way. I can honestly say, I am a much better version of myself after this pilgrimage, and it is my genuine hope that you tap into your best self while reading this book.

The purpose of this book is to take you on a 52-week journey to discovering a happier life. Over the next year, I will share my moments of clarity and offer you space to work through your thoughts on the matter. This book isn't about being right or wrong. Promise me you won't use this book as another reason to beat yourself up! If one of the stories stirs your emotions, ask yourself why? Sit with it. Discomfort is a sign you're getting close to your answer. Use the journaling sections to help you process your thoughts, set weekly goals, spark inspiration in your own life, and unpack the decades of shit that has been dumped on you, one week at a time. There will be questions to guide your journaling and from the surface you could write one-word responses, resist this urge and dig a little deeper. You owe it to yourself to be specific.

Each week there will be a short mantra to help you focus. What is a mantra? How to use it? It's as easy as just repeating it to yourself over and over again. That's what a mantra is. It's a short little saying that we cycle over and over in our minds until we manifest it, until it comes to fruition. As we embark on this adventure together, I want you to know that you are not alone. I am here with you. We have a book club on Facebook if you'd like to join our online community there is a seat for you waiting. Nothing better than linking arms with people going the same direction as you are. We can follow the yellow brick road together.

Search Check up From Your Neck up- Book Club or https://www.face-book.com/groups/413536126011979/

While this book is helping us focus our energy every week, it is important to also hold space for the seasons in our lives, both literal and figurative. Each season has different energetic power. There are four pit-stops for seasonal reflections, and many of the mantras align with the corresponding season. These spaces will allow you to look at the bigger picture. Depending on when you start this journey, you may not be in the season that is being examined, it's your book now, and you can use it however you wish. Feel free to leaf through to the season that applies and begin there instead.

Last thing I want you to remember, you are stronger than you think, and you are loved.

Let's get to work on building that life you've been dreaming of.

Before we jump into the first week, I want to give you your first task. Write a letter to your future self, the person you will be in one year. What are your goals, aspirations, and hopes? What do you want to manifest this year? Who do you want to become? What problems do you want to solve? What hobbies do you want to start? What kind of person does your dog think you are and how can you become more like that? Be detailed; allow yourself to dream big.

WEEK I

BIG TIGERS AND LITTLE MICE

Story Time: This week, I thought I would kick us off by telling you a fun yoga story. It's a story that I tell my yoga students frequently because it's so powerful. A farmer was walking in a large field on his land in Africa, just taking a pleasant stroll. As he walked through the field, he comes across a tiger circling his area. He's cautiously watching the tigers moves. He accidentally makes eye contact with the tiger and realizes that's not a smart idea. You don't make eye contact with a predator that wants to eat you. He slowly begins to back up, the tiger senses his fear and pounces. In a panic, the farmer starts running for dear life while the tiger's chasing him, getting closer and closer. He's running as fast as he can, but up ahead he can see that he is running straight for the edge of a cliff.

He thinks, "oh, my God, I'm going to have to jump off of this ledge or get eaten by a tiger! This is a terrible dilemma."

The farmer runs right up to the ledge and looks over the edge, and he sees a long vine hanging out, and he thinks, "OK, well, at least I'll be

able to jump off the ledge and grab onto this branch, and I'll hold on."
As the tiger was getting close to him, he leaps off the edge and clasps
the branch before plummeting down the ravine. Now he's holding onto
this branch for dear life, and he thinks, "well, maybe I'll hold on for a little bit. The tiger will get bored, and he'll go away." After a few minutes,
he looks up, and the tiger is looking over the edge at him, slapping his
jowls, drooling, waiting, patiently waiting. "Crap," he thinks, "maybe I
can climb down the branch and get down the cliff." He looks down to
plan his escape route but what does he see?

Another tiger circling, waiting, looking up at him, as if to say, "Yeah
buddy, you're about to be a snack."

"Damn, I'm stuck here," he mutters to himself. "I can't climb up. I can't
climb down. I'm just going to hold on, and I'm going to wait for my
family to find me. After a while, they're going to miss me. They're going
to wonder where I am, and they're going to come and find me." He's
resolved to just holding on.

A little time passes, and fatigue is starting to set in. He hears a little
squeaking noise, and he looks up. At the top of his lifeline branch are
two little mice chewing on the twine. "You have got to be kidding me,"
he thinks, "I'm going to die right here, right now. These mice are going
to eat through this vine, I'm going to fall and plummet to my death.
Then still be eaten by a tiger."

He doesn't want to die and realizes he's got to find a way out in order
to survive. He takes a deep breath and starts looking around to see
if there's any way out of this. Out of the corner of his eyes, he sees
a small protruding ledge with a tiny bush and on the shrub is one big
strawberry.

Shifting his grip on the branch with one arm, he leans out as far as
he can to reach the fruit. He's stretching hard to get that strawberry,

plucks the strawberry off the bush, closes his eyes, and puts it in his mouth...this is the sweetest and juiciest strawberry he's ever had in his life.

I told this story to my son, and I asked him, "What do you think the moral of the story is?" He responded, "to always eat because you never know when it's going to be your last meal." And that's true, literal in fact. It's so funny that from the mouth of babes, we find clarity. That's a very good moral, but to me, the moral of this story is that we cannot get away from the tigers and the mice of our lives.

The tiger above the cliff is the past. It's our regrets, our experiences and failures, our trauma, and our memories. It's all of the things that we're running from. The tiger below us represents the fear of the future, the things to come. The things that we worry about—how bad it's going to be and how terrible it's going to be. Even though we don't know what the future holds anxiety still takes over.

The mice symbolize the things that go on in your life that are a little bit smaller, but they annoy the heck out of you, the things that work your last nerve. They chew on your branch (that boss who's a jerk, or how many times you had to tell your husband to take your car for an oil change or, the number of times you ask your kids unload the dish-washer before they actually did it, or the rude customer service person when you call because your bill is wrong). The mice are all the little, insignificant things in your life that annoy you down to your last nerve.

The essence of this story, and what I want you to take with you this week is to broaden your peripherals. There are always going to be times when you feel like you're barely hanging on. If you widen your peripherals, if you look beyond the big tigers and little mice, you will find sweetness in your life.

You will find the strawberries, and at that moment, when you're truly alive, when you're truly awake, you're going to enjoy sweetness like you've never tasted it before.

Now, you know, chances are high that, you're going to be frustrated this week. You're going to be annoyed by something, or your past could creep up and bite you. You could be running from a tiger right now, or you could be dealing with a mouse. Look for the strawberries, find the sweetness because it's there, even if you can't see it right away, sometimes we get so overwhelmed by the burdens of the past and the anxieties of the future and the little mice of our lives that we forget that there is sweetness everywhere, we just have to train ourselves to look for it. Hot cup of coffee, a cold glass of wine, a nice walk where you stop and smell the roses, cuddle time with your pet or take a bubble bath. There are all kinds of ways for you to find sweetness in your life if you open your eyes a little wider and look for it.

WHAT ARE SOME OF THE TIGERS AND MICE YOU HAVE BEEN FACING LATELY?

_____

_____

_____

_____

_____

_____

WHAT WAYS CAN YOU IDENTIFY THE TIGERS AND MICE MORE QUICKLY?

_____

_____

_____

_____

_____

_____

_____

LIST OF STRAWBERRIES YOU FOUND THIS WEEK:

_____

_____

_____

_____

_____

_____

_____

_____

_____

_____

_____

_____

_____

WEEK 2

IT'S RAINING MEN

It's so important that we start to harness our mental power and stop letting our brain run the show because our brain is stupid. Yes, I said it, my brain is dumb. Sometimes it feels like I gave a toddler a Mountain Dew inside my head— sheer chaos.

When you let your brain have free reign, it will think about all the worst things. Have you ever laid in bed at night and heard a plane fly over your house, then you think- what would happen if that plane crashed into my house right now? Then spiral into an entirely made-up story about how you would try to evacuate, which kid you would save first, what you would say to your spouse.

Or here is another one of my favorites. I tried calling my husband, and it goes straight to voicemail. That's odd, I'll think. I hope he's okay, but what if he's not? What if he was in a car accident and is trapped? What if his phone was smashed and the police can't call me? Then call back every few minutes, building myself into a total panic attack that some-thing terrible has happened, only to find out he was in a meeting at work and turned off his phone. I can't be the only one.

You will imagine the worst of the worst, and you will set yourself up for a complete meltdown. It's a safety mechanism we have in our heads called the conscious brain. Your thinking brain is designed to protect you from bad things happening in your life. The part of your mind that says, "don't touch that flame, it will burn you." But what that also means is that it's always on guard.

It's tough because this part of our mind also uses our past experiences to rationalize this thought process. Here is what I mean. I had a friend who got a cute puppy. While she was at work her puppy got a hold of an open potato chip bag. The puppy was small enough to fit his whole head into the bag but couldn't figure out how to get out, and unfortunately suffocated and died. Because my stupid brain knows this story, every time I come home, I immediately start looking for my dog, half expecting to find him in a potato chip bag. Every. Damn. Time.

In basketball there is a technique players use called a pivot. It is a way to get away from an attacking defender. You keep one foot planted and use the other foot to change directions and get away from the other player. This week I want you to practice pivoting in your brain.

When you catch yourself spiraling, just think pivot and intentionally move your thoughts to another subject. One of my go-to tricks is to start singing a song in my mind. I don't like these ugly thoughts, so I start singing 'It's Raining Men'. Why? Because both thought processes are ludicrous only one doesn't make me feel bad. Don't like that song, fine. Choose another one, but make sure it's crazy enough to disrupt your routine thought patterns.

WHAT ARE YOUR LOOPING STORIES?

_____

_____

_____

_____

_____

_____

HOW DID YOU PIVOT THIS WEEK?

_____

_____

_____

_____

_____

_____

_____

_____

_____

WEEK 3

WINTER, SPRING, SUMMER, AND FALL

Story Time- A long time before technology, a father wanted to teach his four sons, a lesson about life. He sent them on a voyage across the valley to view a pear tree. He sent one son during each of the four seasons. After they all returned from their voyage, they all sat down at the table and started to describe what they each experienced while they were there.

The first son who went in winter said, "Oh, I don't know why I had to go view that old dead thing. It was freezing cold, and I got frostbite on my toes. It was just absolutely miserable. The tree looked dead, and there was no life in it. The dark and gloomy days only made the treacherous trip worse. I barely made it back."

The next son who went in spring said, "Well, I didn't experience that at all. The tree was bursting with blossoms and new life. The rain had recently passed, allowing the sun to peek through casting a rainbow off in the distance. Birds were flying around, and it was simply stunning."

The third son who went in the summer said, "Odd, that's not what I experienced either. When I went, it was hot. It was so hot the sun was beating down on my body and my horse. I was exhausted by the time I reached the tree. It had so much foliage, and I was grateful that I could hide under the tree and get some shade. I ended up falling asleep and taking a nap underneath the tree, and it was just delightful to have that tree protect me from the sun."

The last son said, "Interesting enough, I also had a completely different experience. When I went, the tree was overflowing with pears. So many that I brought some back for you guys. They were perfectly ripe and juicy, so I ate to my heart's content."

The father speaks up at this point, "Precisely boys, things change. So many times in our lives, we judge. We judge things based on the season that we encounter them in. We all go through seasons in our life. We learn, grow, shed, and create."

I've been in broke AF seasons where Foodie Friday consisted of a fun game called, how to make a meal for $4. I've been in paycheck to paycheck seasons, using change to pay for gas because my direct deposit hasn't hit. I've been on welfare as a child and felt so ashamed needing WIC after having my first son. I know what it's like to struggle, and if you knew me then, you understand how much I had to do to transform my life.

Contrary to that, many of you are walking into my life right now. You see my season of abundance. You see me driving a Jaguar, owning a beautiful home, and traveling the world. That's because I'm in one of my autumn seasons. Yes, *one* of my autumns. Just like we have four seasons a year and live for many years, life is cyclical. Your life will feel hot and then cold, inspired, and then bored. It will move from poverty to plenty.

Notice when you hear people say things like, "Oh, you know she is so fake, I went on spring break with her. Now she's pretending to be a goody-two-shoes. I went to high school with that girl, and she was a total jerk to everyone." These statements are likely made during the time in which that person was exposed to someone. While they were in their winter.

Here's the thing, people are allowed to change, and just because you knew somebody ten years ago and they were catty, ugly, and or nasty, it doesn't mean they're still that way. The real lesson here is to not cling to tightly to the sweet season and to remember that the bad seasons are temporary. The key to happiness is not letting one season turn into a lifetime of suffering. Allow yourself to go through the cycle, allow yourself to grow, and to get better.

Without plantings seeds in the spring, watering & weeding in the summer, you won't be able to have an abundant fall. All of this is about changing and we resist change. We hate it. We don't want other people to change because it means that we have to change, or it shines a mirror on what we're *not* doing. Unfortunately, everything changes regardless of our feelings. The sooner you can embrace the cycle, the less stress you're going to have inside of your life, the less frustration you're going to have when you stop resisting.

When you stop fighting and you just let yourself move, grow, and breathe, you let those around you do that as well. You will notice a lightness in your heart. You will feel an excitement and energy moving into the next season. You'll think, *"Oooo, what's coming up next?* You'll weather the winters better because you've had the bright spring, warm summer, and fruitful fall.

WHAT SEASON DO YOU THINK YOU ARE IN, AND WHY?

_____

_____

_____

_____

_____

_____

CAN YOU RECALL A SEASON THAT TESTED YOU? HOW DID YOU GET THROUGH IT?

_____

_____

_____

_____

_____

_____

_____

CAN YOU FIND A TIME WHEN THINGS WERE OVERFLOWING? HOW DID THAT FEEL?

SEASONAL REFLECTION:
WINTER

MANTRA:
*Your relationship with yourself sets the tone
for every relationship you have.*

Winter brings closure to the life cycle. Many elements go into hiber-
nation or lay dormant under the earth. Likewise, our social circles
shrink as the cold weather drives us indoors, and we become hermits.
We layer on the clothing to protect against the cold, but be mindful
that it also restricts us from moving freely. Many people (including
me) struggle with the "winter blues." Keep in mind self-care is most
important when we are at our lowest emotional and energetic states.
This is a fantastic time to go inside yourself, do your soul searching,
and work out your shit.

SUGGESTED READING:
- Girl Wash Your Face- Rachel Hollis
- You Are A Badass- Jen Sincero

Don't forget to join our on-line family for even more motivational and
inspirational content. Search Check up From Your Neck up- Book Club
or https://www.facebook.com/groups/413536126011979/

SEASONAL REFLECTION: WINTER

LIST 3 WAYS YOU CAN PRACTICE SELF-CARE:

_____

_____

_____

_____

HOW HAVE PAST WINTERS IMPACTED ME?

_____

_____

_____

_____

WHAT IS MY MENTAL AND EMOTIONAL STATE IN THIS SEASON?

_____

_____

_____

_____

WEEK 4

JUST BREATHE

Did you know the average person takes more than 20,000 breaths per day? It's a pretty magnificent miracle that our bodies continue to breathe even when we aren't awake. Throughout your day, chances are you don't even notice your breath. It just happens naturally. Unless you have a cough, are running a race, or doing some other physical activity, you could go weeks without paying attention to your inhale and exhale.

I want to not only inspire you along our journey together but also offer you some tools to use. Breathing techniques are one of the most powerful tools I have learned to help navigate the day to day stressors life puts on us. Can you think about a time when you were emotionally worked up, lump in your throat, face burning, tears welling? What else are you doing? Holding your breath!

In yoga, the Sanskrit word for breath, which also means life force, is prana. When you are in an emotional storm and holding your breath, you are literally stopping your life force. The same thing goes when we hyperventilate. We have lost total control of our faculties. Every organ in our body needs oxygen to survive, and one of the most critical is our brain.

When the brain doesn't receive sufficient oxygen, it begins to shut down, directly impacting your motor skills and decision-making abilities. You may also start to experience memory loss, and eventually, it escalates to seizures, coma, or death. I know that's a little extreme, but my point is that the breath is a powerful component to our health and welfare. We need to pay closer attention to something with that much power.

This week our mantra is "Just Breathe." Become a student of your breath. Check-in with yourself several times a day and notice the variances. How does your breath feel when you first wake up, when you're at work, the gym, in traffic? Do you see a difference when you're angry versus happy? How does it feel when you hold your breath, how long can you hold it? What does it feel like when you hold your breath in on the inhale and out on the exhale?

All of these subtle variances will help you understand your breathing habits better. When we know better, we do better. Below are a few breathing techniques you can use to become more disciplined in your breath and calm the mind when you are stressed out.

TO HELP YOUR FOCUS:
ALTERNATE NOSTRIL BREATH

When you're feeling scatterbrained, and having difficulty staying on task, try this breath. This breathing technique will balance the two hemispheres of the brain to help you regain your focus. This is great for busy work deadlines or household organization days.

Sit tall in a comfortable place. Hold out your dominant hand and press the tips of your pointer and middle fingers into your palm, leaving your ring finger, pinky finger, and thumb extended.

Bring your hand up in front of your face and press your thumb on the outside of one nostril. Inhale deeply through your open nostril. At the top of your inhalation, release your thumb, press your ring finger on the outside of your other nostril, and exhale. The next inhale will occur on the ring finger side, and the exhale on the thumb side. Repeat several times, finishing with your final exhale on the thumb side.

For added clarity, try holding the breath in and/or out of the body at the top and the bottoms of your breaths. Holding on the inhale will allow you to notice what it feels like to be full. Holding on the exhale will teach you what it feels like to be empty. Both of these extremes are important.

Pro-Tip: Everyone screws this up, so don't stress, just keep going until you find your rhythm.

TO HELP WITH SLEEP:
4-7-8 BREATH

This breath will come in handy when your brain is wide awake, but your body is ready for bed. Highlight this page for the nights when you find yourself replaying unhelpful or painful memories, or the nights when you can't stop worrying about what could go wrong.

Begin by sitting or lying down in a comfortable position. Your eyes can be open or closed. Press the tip of your tongue to the roof of your mouth, slightly open your mouth, and exhale until you reach the bottom of your breath.

Close your mouth and quietly inhale through your nose for four counts.

Then hold your breath for seven counts. Finally, exhale very slowly so that it takes a total of eight counts to return to the bottom of your breath.

Pro-tip: Diffusing some lavender or other soothing essential oils can help you create an even more relaxing sleeping space.

TO HELP RELAX
COUNTDOWN BREATH

This breath is perfect for when you want to flip the eff out. When you can feel your blood boiling, or if you are feeling the onset of anxiety, this breath will calm the storm.

Find a quiet place, outside if possible, fresh air has magical properties. For days when you only have a minute start from ten, take a deep inhale through the nose, then take a sighing exhale out of the mouth. Repeat until you count down to one. If you're in a car or have more time, try starting from twenty.

Pro-tip: Think in your brain the word "relax" with every inhale this will remind yourself of what your goal is.

WEEK 5

DIRTY WINDOWS

Story Time: Shortly after getting married, the newlyweds bought a new house and started the hustle and bustle of moving in and unboxing their possessions. After a long day of unpacking, the couple sat down to have their first dinner in their new dining room. As they're sitting in their dining room eating, the wife looks out the windows, and she sees her new neighbor hanging up her laundry old school style on a clothesline, and the wife thinks, *"why is her laundry so dirty?"*

A couple of days go by, and now they're having breakfast on a Sunday morning in their dining room, and she looks out. Again, her neighbor is hanging up her dirty laundry. The wife turns to her husband and says, "babe, have you seen how dirty the neighbor's laundry is? Why doesn't she know how to wash it properly?"

It takes a few more days until the wife can finally hang up some curtains in the dining room, and as she's working, she can't help but gaze out at her odd neighbor hanging up more dirty laundry. The wife thinks to herself, *"man she must not know how to wash clothes the right way I should show her what my mom taught me to use because maybe she didn't have a proper home training and she needs somebody to help her out."*

The following weekend the wife had some errands to run. She comes home later that day and begins unloading everything from the store in the dining room. Something catches her eye- the neighbor is out hanging her laundry again, but this time it's all clean, white as white can be. "Hey babe," she calls to her husband in the other room, "did you see the lady next door finally figured out how to wash her laundry the right way?"

After unpacking, she peeked into the other room and asked her husband, "so would you do while I was gone, babe?" The husband says, "I washed the windows."

We've all been told not to judge others under the pretense that we don't know what others are going through. This story is so important in our lives because it challenges the way we view the world.

This story is about the filters that we have on over our own eyes and the way that we see things. We judge people based on where we grew up, how our parents raised us, and our religion. We judge them based on our prejudices and our own experiences. Every single one of those things is just a filter. As a result, we don't see things as they are, we see them as we are. Not judging other people isn't just about giving them a pass because you don't know what they've been through but also understanding that we see things through dirty windows.

Right now, I'm looking outside, and I see spots all over my windows. I don't have a clear picture. I have a diluted picture of how I think it should look like outside. That's one of the reasons why I come on Facebook Live for the Monday Mantra with no makeup on and sometimes without even my teeth brushed because I want you to see a clearer picture of who I am. Facebook is so dangerous for that very reason, everything is filtered. Each image you see has been buffed and shined up so that it seems perfect. Be cautious to not get disillusioned of what reality looks like.

As you move through your week, pay close attention to the filters you're viewing the world with. Notice when you're driving down the street and you see someone standing on the side of the road with a cardboard sign. What is your first thought? I guarantee you it's got a filter on it. If we've been told that homeless people are fakers and that they're greedy or that they're lazy or that they don't know how to get a job then immediately when you see someone standing with a sign on the side of the road you are seeing them through that filter. You have no idea what they've been going through. But more importantly how can you see this situation more clearly?

WHAT IS A TIME IN YOUR LIFE WHEN
YOU THOUGHT SOMETHING WAS ONE WAY,
AND LEARNED LATER IT WASN'T THAT WAY AT ALL?

_____

_____

_____

_____

_____

_____

HAVE YOU EVER MISJUDGED SOMEONE?

_____

_____

_____

_____

_____

_____

WEEK 6

I WILL NOT BE
MY OWN WORST ENEMY

So many times in our lives, we look to other people for validation. We seek other people to co-sign on our decisions. It's because we've forgotten how to trust ourselves. I think the number one reason why we don't believe ourselves is because of that nasty self-talk that we do, that constant self-deprecation, that consistent putting ourselves down and telling ourselves we're not capable, we're not competent. But why would you trust a person that talks to you like that? You are right not to trust that person. That person is a liar. That person does not believe in you, and the negative voice will wreak havoc on your life if you let it. This inner voice is loud and will quickly become so dominant in your thoughts that you think it is the "real" you.

Good news though friends! There is a deeper part of you that supports you and wants you to be successful, but we've forgotten how to listen. It's hard because this second voice only whispers and the first voice shouts. We just need to learn how to tap into that whispering voice again, because instead, we're looking to other people. Folks that may not have our best interest at heart, they have their own shit they're working through, their battles with insecurities and their predisposed ideas on what *they* can or cannot do. These are problems they will gladly transfer onto you; they may not be the best source of guidance when it comes to making choices in our lives.

I found it helpful to identify and name the negative voice so I could start recognizing it when it flared up. Naming it also allowed me to disconnect from it as being a part of me. Once it became a separate thing in my mind it was easier to turn it off, in fact, full transparency here my negative voice is named Sharon (no offense to all the Sharons out there), and when I hear it telling me I'm not a good writer or to eat that second donut, I say "shut up Sharon" and then redirect my thoughts to more supportive themes. I named it Sharon because I am a nerd at heart that loves alliterations- Monday Mantra, Foodie Friday, and Shutup Sharon.

This week, my hope for you as part of your mantra is to practice trusting yourself, start drinking your own Kool-Aid, to believe in yourself and to go out there and do some amazing shit with your life. It's going to be a great week. If you put on those positivity goggles and say, you know what, I'm capable of doing more and I don't need anyone else's approval. I don't need anyone else to co-sign on my life. I don't need anyone else to hold my hand as I make this happen. You have everything you need inside of you if you're just willing to listen to it, if you're just brave enough to get out there and trust your gut instinct and all the gifts that you've been given.

WHAT NAME ARE YOU GOING TO LABEL YOUR NEGATIVE VOICE?

_____

_____

_____

_____

_____

WHAT IS A TIME IN YOUR LIFE WHEN TRUSTING SOMEONE ELSE'S GUIDANCE BACKFIRED?

_____

_____

_____

_____

_____

_____

_____

WHAT IS A TIME IN YOUR LIFE WHEN YOU TRUSTED YOUR GUT AND IT PAID OFF?

WEEK 7

YOU DON'T OWN ME

Painful pasts haunt us all. I don't know a single person who hasn't experienced some form of grief, heartache, loss, or trauma. It wasn't until recently I felt comfortable even talking about my past. It was a dark, dirty secret that I kept locked away deep down inside. "If I pretend it doesn't exist, it will go away, I would think to myself." "Conceal, don't feel," an inspiring princess once said. I felt that.

For as long as I can remember, I have despised the winter. I loathe being cold. I usually dip down into the winter blues, despite how good things are in my life. I can't shake this nagging sadness that takes over this time of year. This emotional instability is something I had accepted as part of myself until I decided to do the hard work of unpacking my feelings around it.

Just because the pain is in the past, doesn't mean it doesn't continue to impact you today. I know this because I keep finding hang-ups directly tied to my abuse. My stepfather was in construction, that means his work was seasonal, spring through fall were prime working conditions.

Growing up in Ohio there were lots of snowstorms, so working wasn't an option in construction. What does that mean? He was home more.

There it is— my light bulb of clarity. The hang-up is glaring at me in the face now. The season is directly linked to my memories and I hate the winter because most of my abuse occurred during this time. The cold is a trigger that takes me right back to being that vulnerable little girl every time the temperatures drop.

Rape, divorce, death, sickness, abuse, abortion, drugs, and any other negative memory you're holding on to is what we are facing this week. This is the most difficult work you will do, mainly because we've got a death grip on our memories and can't "let it go." We're holding on to those terrible memories with everything we've got. It's suffocating us, and because we've been clinging to them so tightly, we believe it is part of our identity.

Here is where my mantra for the week comes in: You Don't Own Me! This is what I shout every time I find a hang-up. This is the war cry I use to take back my life. It fires me up to cut those strings my abuser still has on me, to challenge myself to protect my emotions and not get down in the winter. I want to find beauty in this season because he is not allowed to take anything else from me. He does not own me!

I use this mantra to disrupt the negative thought patterns. I scream it with a rebel yell. Your past does not own you. Your pain doesn't own you.

Even if you feel that person doesn't deserve forgiveness, you should forgive because you deserve peace. Many of us are not moving forward in our lives because we can't let go of the past. You weren't meant to carry the mountain. You were only expected to climb it. Stop using your past as a reason why you can't succeed in your life and start using it as your reason to exceed all odds.

HOW IS YOUR PAST IMPACTING
YOUR PRESENT-DAY?

_____

_____

_____

_____

_____

_____

WHAT HAVE YOU LET "OWN" YOU IN THE PAST?

_____

_____

_____

_____

_____

WHERE THERE ANY TIMES THIS WEEK WHEN YOU NEEDED A PASS?

WEEK 8
STOP DIGGING SHALLOW WELLS

Story Time: There once was a guy who bought a piece of land and needed to dig a well in his yard to get running water on his property. One day he heads out with his shovel and starts digging, he gets about four or five feet down, but he doesn't strike any water. "Must be a bad spot?" he says to himself as he climbs out of the hole. He paces 20 feet, decides this must be a better spot and starts digging again. He digs down four or five feet but no water. "That's frustrating," he thinks as he realizes all this effort is making him thirsty, he's got to strike water soon, right? He climbs out, walks 20 feet in another direction and he starts digging another hole.

Dry! Annoyed now and incredibly parched he is determined to find water, so he digs another shallow hole only to again come up empty handed. He feverishly gets out, paces 20 feet in the opposite direction, and digs another hole for five feet. No water. He continues to do this all day long. He burrows 20 to 30 holes in his yard, and he never found any water. By the time the sun is setting, he's exhausted, he has no fruits from his labor, and he's thirsty. So thirsty.

I absolutely love the story I just told you because it perfectly illustrates the many times we quit something half way through, when it gets just a bit too hard, when we feel like we've worked but we don't have any fruits. We don't know for sure if digging more will result in getting what we want. We tell ourselves that it's easier to get out and go somewhere else.

We think, "Look, the grass is greener over there. I should go over there. Susie had results, maybe I will too. Let me just go from this company to this company to this company, because I've been here for a few months and still haven't been promoted. Let me go from this relationship to this relationship to this relationship because things got too complicated this one and being together shouldn't be this hard."

We end up digging shallow holes for everything in our life, only to bail for the next big thing. As a result, we never get to manifest anything extraordinary because we don't know how to keep working. When times get hard, we throw up our hands and we move on. Unfortunately, so many of us are taking this unfulfilling approach to life and feel like we're repeatedly failing, which only adds insult to injury.

A majority of the good things I've received in life have been from the times I've worked my hardest. Do you have fitness goals? You work out for a week or two and don't see any results, so you think, "must not be the right thing for me." Then, we hop from Whole 30, to Keto, to diet pills looking for an easier fix. This hopping only creates a yo-yo in your metabolism creating a vicious cycle. If you're working out two to three times a week, try increasing that to five, or six days *and* adding better nutrition management to see results. Dig deeper, don't give up. We want to be building deep wells that are full of so much water that we can share it with the world. That can only happen if we commit to seeing our goals through.

Your gifts that are inside of you are buried under years of dirt and you've got to keep digging in order to discover them. You can't just scratch the surface and expect to manifest something amazing. You have to put some blood, some sweat, and some tears into your life if you really want something great to come out.

This week, the mantra is going to challenge you to dig a little deeper as you move through your week. As you start coming in contact with resistance, like a bit of shade from your friends because you're staying late to work on a project, or a partner bailing on their part, or perhaps missing a deadline, I want you to remember the words: I'm going to dig a little deeper. Remember to keep pushing. Don't quit because your blessings are on the other side of the struggle. Everything that you want in your life is on the other side of the battle, but if you don't go through it, you can't have it.

There are no ifs, and, or buts. I wish this weren't true, I've prayed for easier options, but the only way to it, is through it. There's no easy path to life. There's going to be a lot of rejection; people won't understand your vision, you're not going to win the lottery. You will wake up and have struggles, expect them. When they come, you don't have to freak out because it's part of the process. You've got to be willing to push through and quit digging shallow wells in your life. Think about all the things that you've started that you've never followed through on. Think about all the things that you've done and quit before it was ever successful because it was just too hard. Shiny ball syndrome is real.

Stop the pattern of quitting and start committing to yourself to follow through. What would happen if just this one time you didn't quit on yourself? You will show yourself you are capable of going deeper, you will learn lessons, and build confidence. You will learn that your word means something, and when you say you'll do it, you do!

WHAT ARE YOUR GOALS THIS WEEK?

_____

_____

_____

_____

_____

_____

WHAT CAN YOU DO TO KEEP PUSHING WHEN IT GETS HARD?

_____

_____

_____

_____

_____

_____

WHAT WILL IT FEEL LIKE TO CHECK THESE THINGS OFF YOUR LIST?

WEEK 9

THERE ARE NO VICTIMS

The mantra this week may trigger something as you read it but remember that feeling that is bubbling inside of you is a sign, that you need to process something new. New thoughts and growth always feel a little uncomfortable. *There are no victims.* That is the mantra for the week. When I say that, I know a lot of you probably recoil thinking there *are* victims in the world. While I can agree that many people have bad things happen to them, it doesn't mean they're victims.

Bad things happen all the time- a Soldier loses their leg in the war, a teen gets in a car accident with a drunk driver, a young college fresh-men gets raped at a frat party, or someone finds out they have cancer. We can all agree terrible things happen, and I certainly have tons of compassion for folks going through these things. However, I'm going to say that being a victim is a mindset. There is no such thing as a real victim out there. You are only a victim if you choose to be a victim. So, think about your life. Are you walking around saying, "oh, poor, pitiful me" like Eeyore from Winnie the Pooh? That is a victim mindset, you are using your life's experiences as a crutch, and you'll know you're doing it if you have said: "oh I can't do that because <insert terrible thing> happened."

Real Talk: The moment you get through that terrible situation, you are a survivor. You are a victor. You have proven that you are resilient that and you are capable of getting through some of the hardest shit life can throw at you. Stop acting weak. Stop pretending like that's the end of your life. You've got a chance to use that story to fuel you, to move into something else, to manifest something better, to be a testimony and a lighthouse to the other people in the world going through the same thing. You already survived, and being a victim is just a story we use to excuse our current situation.

Let me share a little bit about my story from when I was a child; I was sexually abused by my stepdad from the time I was four until I was twelve. It was a nightmare of a life. I lived through hell for eight years, which is almost 3,000 days of my life. When I finally started telling people about what I had been through, everyone's response was "Oh, my God, Marie, I never would have guessed that you had been through something like that."

Do you know why they would say that? It was because I wasn't walking around with my tail between my legs like the whole world was against me. Instead I was empowered to realize that I was a survivor, not a victim. By choosing the pain, you give it more power to hurt you over and over again. You are giving that situation *more* control. You are giving that person who hurt you a voice in your future because they are continuing to hurt you and continuing to stop your growth every single day. Let go of the memories, reliving them does not serve you.

That awful thing that happened to you is not the last bad thing that could ever happen to you in your life, but now you have proof you can get through painful situations. The moment you get through that situation, you have proven that you are resilient. The moment that situation doesn't kill you, you have demonstrated that you are strong enough to handle it and rise above it.

WRITE YOUR STORY. PUTTING IT ON PAPER ALLOWS YOU TO PROCESS THE PAIN.

_____

_____

_____

_____

_____

_____

WHAT WOULD YOU TELL SOMEONE THAT IS GOING THROUGH THE SAME SITUATION? HOW COULD YOU USE YOUR PAST TO INSPIRE SOMEONE ELSE TO KEEP GOING?

_____

_____

_____

_____

WEEK 10

ASSUME NO BAD INTENT

The mantra for this week is to assume no bad intent. What does that mean? Well, I feel like we generally walk around feeling like everyone is out to get us. Always on the defense, because we're confident people are intentionally trying to piss us off. I noticed a massive shift in my life when I started assuming no bad intent. In fact, most people are not thinking about you. You are not at the forefront of their minds. When you get your feelings hurt because somebody did something, it's probably unintentional. They didn't do it on purpose. They weren't trying to be a *Dirk*.

For those of you that don't know, a Dirk is a word that I created. It's a mix of dick and jerk. It's kind of like a hybrid word, and I want to make it a thing. So whenever I say Dirk, you know what I mean, and I encourage you to use it freely when you cross paths with them in the wild.

Most people aren't out there trying to "get to you," trying to hurt your feelings, or trying to offend you. Most times I would wager, they're not even thinking about you at all.

I can ask my husband to take my car for an oil change seven or eight times over several weeks. When not done, it feels like a personal attack, a complete disregard for my request. Using this week's mantra helped me realize he isn't neglecting my request on purpose. He's not trying to start a fight. He gets distracted, or he gets busy, or he forgets. Now that I realize he's not trying to hurt, I'm able to let it go a little bit easier. I'm not burying it deep down inside of me, and letting it fester into resentment.

When I make plans to go out with a friend, and she shows up late, she wasn't doing it on purpose. She wasn't saying my time doesn't matter. She showed up late because something else was going on in her life. Maybe there was traffic, or her kids were sick. When somebody doesn't answer your phone call, it doesn't mean that you pissed them off and they don't like you anymore. Perhaps their phone died, or they dropped it in the toilet. When you assume no ill intent, you give people a pass to make mistakes and be human.

The golden adage of treat others the way that you want to be treated is so critical here because I know there are lots of times when I am not trying to hurt anybody's feelings, but it happens. And I want a pass. I want a pass when I show up late to something because of traffic, I want somebody to forgive me and show me some grace when I can't deliver on what I promise.

So, if I want somebody to show me that kind of grace, shouldn't I extend that same in return? Assume no bad intent, friends, as you move through your week. Nobody is out to get you. Nobody is intentionally trying to ruin your day. Give them a little bit of grace and give yourself a little bit of peace by deciding that they're not trying to hurt you.

Maybe start to fill in the blanks with a new understanding. Instead of saying, "oh, she's a b@#$%. She's just totally trying to hurt my feelings"

Think, instead "oh, my God, she must be having a terrible day." When I started this with my husband, it transformed our relationship. I am not as nit-picky anymore. Once it worked in one area, I started extending it all around me.

I hear people talking negatively about somebody else; I find myself giving them grace. I find myself saying, well, maybe they were having a bad day, or perhaps they were running late. Or I become the devil's advocate. I'm giving everybody a chance to make a mistake without having to be the bad guy or the villain. There are no villains. Everybody is just trying to do their best. Sometimes our crap bleeds over, but you should not get butt hurt because it sometimes impacts you. Nobody is trying to hurt you on purpose.

Assume no bad intent. Nobody is out to get you. Nobody wants to ruin your day. As you move through your week, look for those opportunities to extend some grace, to be merciful and forgiving to the people in your lives, especially the people who are closest to you. You already know they love you. Why would somebody that loves you try to hurt you on purpose? They're not. And since they're not doing it on purpose, give them a pass.

DID YOU MEET ANY DIRKS THIS WEEK?

_____

_____

_____

_____

_____

_____

HOW WERE YOU ABLE TO REFRAME
THE INTERACTION AND EXTEND GRACE?

_____

_____

_____

_____

_____

_____

_____

HOW CAN YOU LET IT GO?

WEEK II
ATTITUDE OF GRATITUDE

This week we are going H.A.M. on the checkup part of this book. I've noticed that lately when I start talking to people, everything they have to say is very negative. Everywhere I turn, people are complaining. I'm not saying life is good for everybody all the time and you shouldn't tell people about your problems, but I wanted to give you some perspective. This week, we're going to talk about the attitude of gratitude because it makes a massive impact on your life. If you find yourself in a storm, you need to stop and create a gratitude list immediately.

The universal law of attraction states: what you focus on expands. If you're spending all your time focused on how bad life is and how hard the struggles are and how much you're suffering, then guess what? You're going to get more suffering and even more struggles. Don't waste any more energy! Don't give any more of your time to those negative circumstances. Become a steward of what puts you on tilt so you can hone in on what's triggering you as soon as possible. Only then you can stop it from getting worse.

You can't change every crappy thing that happens, but you have control of what goes on right between your ears. Yes, devastating things happen to people all the time, and everybody suffers. I suffer, and I have bad days, but you won't ever see me moaning and groaning about it.

This week, your attitude adjustment starts with a daily practice of focusing on the good things in your life, the things that make you smile, and bring you joy. All I want you to start doing is writing down what you're grateful for. What are you thankful for in your life? Be specific.

I listed each person in my family. Why? Because I'm grateful for them for different reasons. I'm thankful for each person in my life for the insight and unconditional love they offer. I'm grateful for each of my jobs. Why? I've learned something from every business decision. When we learn, we grow.

Everything that provides value to your life gets written down on this list. In the beginning, it might be pretty straightforward. You might find yourself writing down just the basics: Mom, Pop, pup, home, etc. You hit the obvious ones quickly, but then it gets a little harder.

Here are my top tips for making a bigger list.

1. Be Specific: I added wine as it adds value to my life. Then I included coffee on my list too. You know why? Because it's fueling my life force and I don't see how you decaffeinated people do it.

2. Branch Off: Once you think of one thing, then you think of another—case in point Tip 1. Obviously, I love my beverages. Shout out to H2O!

3. Look Forward: Gratitude for blessings that are yet to come is the highest form of faith. Manifest the life you want by envisioning it into your life and what it would feel like to have that.

4. Phone a Friend: I am always so inspired listening to other people's gratitude list. Gratitude lists are the new Christmas Wish List! Asking your friend is simple with a subtle tweak in your daily interactions. Instead of asking *what's up*, ask *what's good*? Get people thinking and talking about the good.

When you sit back at the end of that five minutes each day this week, allow yourself to take it in. I'm guessing you are immediately going to feel overwhelmed with gratitude and gratitude invites abundance. Isn't that what you want? You want to invite better things into your life. You want to invite in positivity. You want to start to manifest amazing things that you can be proud of in your life.

So that when somebody asks you later this week, how are you doing? You could say, I'm blessed. Even better, I'm abundantly blessed rather than, you know, the same old shit, different day. Who do you want to hang out with? The person that's abundantly blessed or the person that's walking around saying, same old shit, different day. I want to be around the abundantly blessed people, and that's how you start. It is with a list of gratitude. Flip the switch of negativity in your mind.

WHAT ARE YOU GRATEFUL FOR THIS WEEK?

SUNDAY

_____

_____

_____

MONDAY

_____

_____

_____

TUESDAY

_____

_____

_____

WEDNESDAY

_____

_____

_____

THURSDAY

_____

_____

_____

FRIDAY

_____

_____

_____

SATURDAY

_____

_____

_____

WEEK 12

CUPS OR COFFEE?

Story Time: A bunch of college alumni were meeting with their old professor to catch up on life after graduation. Not too long into the conversation, the former students began to moan and groan about life, their new professions, and what they're doing with their careers. After listening earnestly to the students gripe for a little while, the professor goes into the kitchen to make a pot of coffee, and he quickly realizes he doesn't have enough coffee cups for all.

The professor scours the kitchen and he puts out an assembly of mix-matched coffee cups. He puts out delicate crystal cups and the fine China cups from his grandmother. He puts out big cups, little cups. He puts out ceramic mugs and plastic cups. Lastly, he finds a couple of Styrofoam cups to make sure that everybody can have coffee.

After setting out the coffee and cups with other various coffee supplies, the professor sends the students to pick their cups and they all comply happily, fill up their coffee mugs then sit back down. As he scans the table, he notices that the only cups that are left are the cheap cups, the Styrofoam cups, and the plastic cups. Every one of the students took the nice cups, the ceramic, crystal, and the fine China ones were all claimed. He looks at the students, gets very serious, and he says, "maybe this is your problem."

"Maybe you're so focused on the kind of cup that you have, you aren't paying attention to the coffee, because the container does not impact the quality of the coffee. The cup does not change the flavor nor add any value to the coffee. Yet, when you were left to your own devices, you intentionally chose the highest quality cup. And what's even worse," he continues, "after you decided on your cup, you started eyeing each other's. 'His is prettier, oh I wish I had one like hers.' "

This concept is likely true in our lives, as well. We say, *oh, look at the house she has, I wanted a house like that. Look at his job; I should have had a situation like that. Wow, look at her rocking that incredible dress. I wish I could wear something like that.* The cup doesn't change what is on the inside, just like your job, car, house, even your physical body doesn't speak to the quality of person you are.

We get so distracted by these material things, by the vessels that we forget that the true essence of who we are and what we have to give are our talents, generosity, and our compassion. Our ability to live in this world has nothing to do with how much money we make the size of the house that we live in, the kind of car we drive, whether we weigh 500 pounds or whether we weigh a 100 pounds.

Sparkly cups are everywhere but don't mistake the cup for the coffee. Who you are, your essence, your spirit is your coffee. The good stuff inside does not change based on your financial status, or based on your education level. Don't get distracted by the coffee cups.

As you move through your week, look for the things that nourish you, that warm you, that energize you, your passions, your talents, the things that excite you. Focus on what truly matters, and you will feel your level of discontent drop dramatically.

HOW WERE YOU ABLE TO DIFFERENTIATE THE COFFEE FROM THE CUPS THIS WEEK?

_____

_____

_____

_____

_____

_____

HOW DID THIS REFRAME MAKE YOU FEEL?

_____

_____

_____

_____

_____

_____

WEEK 13

COLOR OUTSIDE THE LINES

I was thinking about how I grew up this week, the kind of house where kids were supposed to be seen and not heard. I'm sure many of you know what I am talking about and probably grew up in homes like that too.

Discipline was the name of the game, and many sentences started with "go get me a switch." Kids were supposed to fall in line. We were supposed to sit quietly, not make too much noise. Parents expected us to walk a certain way and talk a certain way. We could only listen to a certain kind of music. We were supposed to go to the church, and no matter what, we were *never* to embarrass our parents in public.

As a parent, I am all for teaching children manners and what it means to be respectful of others, but sometimes the rules I grew up with felt very arbitrary. For example, I wasn't allowed to shave my legs until I was 14, and only during basketball season to prevent further teasing. I wasn't allowed to wear makeup until I was 16, (I still tried to sneak it though,) and I wasn't allowed to get my license until I turned 18, in spite of being an employed, hard-working, straight-A student.

You're told you must get excellent grades and go to college. Once accepted into college, you have to pick a respectable major, preferably the same one as your parents. Only after you graduate can you consider dating, and when you've dated the socially acceptable amount of time, can you get married.

You're now on track to have 2.5 kids, and buy your starter home with a white picket fence. You're expected to get a reliable job with a 401K matching program. Then you should spend 30 years of your life there so that you can get a pension or some kind of retirement plan. Maybe by the time you're 60 or 70 years old, perhaps you can retire.

Your whole life has been mapped out for you from the time you're born. Everybody's been telling you who you're supposed to be, and how you're expected to act. Then you sprinkle in this perfectionist society that we live in with social media, movies, and music videos. All of the airbrushing and photoshopping sets up a breeding ground of shame when we don't fit the mold.

These two forces combined, the militant parenting and the unattainable societal standard, have us feeling lost and disconnected. You can't act like that, and you shouldn't do that. Don't sing in the hallways, be quiet. Walk in straight a line and never color outside the lines. If it's not perfect, you won't be loved, or at least that is how I felt.

There's nothing right about me. I'm never going to live up to those standards. If I can't do it correctly, I shouldn't even attempt it. And so we all just walk around shamefully hiding ourselves. It's amazing how many people are living unfulfilled lives because they are battling the number one fear that we face as people, what other people think about us. Judgment is everywhere; you're damned if you do, and damned if you don't. We've got zero control over it, and we still give it all the power. We stop ourselves from living because we're so worried about what other people think about us.

If you're in America you know, we have a big annual holiday called the 4th of July or Independence Day. It's all about celebrating our freedoms and liberties, our right to vote, and our freedom of speech. We are touted as the "Land of the free." But many of us living in this country are not free because we've forgotten the second part—to be brave. These fearful mindsets bind us; we're living these small, pointless lives to keep the peace. That's not freedom. Freedom is allowing yourself to be everything that you are and being unashamed of it.

Embrace your quirks. I love yoga, but when I first started yoga teacher training, I battled questions like- *you're still going to have a "real" job right? You can't possibly make enough money doing that*. I also fought my ego and struggled by having my worth wrapped up in my job title. Self-doubt tried to creep in—*people won't take you seriously. Who are you to teach anyone anything? You're too introverted to talk to a room of students*. It was anxiety tied directly to the fear of stepping out of line.

Up until that point, I accepted this little box that society wanted me to be in—a small corporate America box. Had I continued on that path; I wouldn't have discovered that I was the kind of person capable of doing a podcast, or speaking on stage in front of hundreds of people. I wouldn't have known that I could slay a winged eyeliner, put my feet behind my head, and be brave enough to share my story of abuse. I wouldn't have known that I had all of that inside me.

That all changes when we stop living in fear of what other people think about us. That's their problem, not yours. Be brave! If your friends and your family are judging you, they are doing so selfishly. The people who matter don't care. The people who care don't matter. That's real freedom.

WHAT ARE 3 THINGS YOU'VE ALWAYS WANTED TO DO?

_____

_____

_____

_____

_____

_____

WHY HAVEN'T YOU STARTED?

_____

_____

_____

_____

_____

_____

DO YOU KNOW ANYONE WHO IS WALKING IN THEIR TRUTH?

WEEK 14

TIME TO DETOX

I think my cell phone is making me dumb. No, seriously. I come from a generation, where we had to use our brains to do basic things like remember phone numbers and figure out how to get from point A to point B. If we had to do a paper in high school, we had to take our happy asses to the library and do some research. I'm blaming Google. They replaced the Dewey Decimal System and we suddenly had unlimited access to information, no brain power required.

It's unfortunate because, as a whole, our society is not using our brains enough. We are allowing our electronics to think for us. We are letting our cell phones drive for us. We are choosing our devices to fill the space, the quiet space. What happens is, our big, beautiful brains never have time to think things through? We never exercise that big sexy muscle that's beneath our scalp.

Why do we have our best ideas when we're in the shower? Simple, we're not distracted. What happens when you're bored? You pick up your phone; you check your email, your messages, you check Facebook, hours lost on Pinterest, and you're reading cat memes. Instead we could be learning how to let our brain sit with itself, learning how to listen to our own thoughts, learning how to be quiet and figure out what's in that noggin.

I work three jobs, one office job done mostly at a computer and two other businesses that require a lot of online marketing. I desperately needed to find ways to unplug; I started doing a 30-minute cell phone detox in the morning when I wake up, and do it before I do anything else. It just allows my brain time to wake up and to set my intention for the day. Why did I implement this change and make it the first thing I do? I realized I'm addicted to my phone because immediately upon waking, I reach for my phone, it is the first thing on my mind..

Why does my cell phone come before kissing my babies? Why does my cell phone come before saying good morning to my husband and making coffee? Why does my cell phone come before peeing or brushing my teeth or petting my puppy? It shouldn't, but it does. So, I drew a line in the sand, or as I like to call it, a healthy boundary. My cell phone should not take priority over those other things.

The moment I pick up my phone, I start downloading everything else into my brain. People sent me messages, a bunch of emails are waiting, and don't even get me started on why the trolls only come out at night. It can set the entire tone of your day if the first thing you input into your brain is work or drama. You have set your day off on the wrong foot.

This week the challenge is to set yourself up properly by giving yourself 15 to 30 minutes of a cell phone detox? Spend that time asking: What do I want to do with my day? Do I want to be productive? Do I want to be a servant leader? Do I want to be happy? What are my goals? By setting that tone everything that comes in after won't have the same negative impact because you've already given yourself the time to use your beautiful brain to determine how your day is going to go?

Don't think you need a cell phone detox? If it hurts to go without anything for an extended amount of time, you might be attached. Some of you are already panicking. Calm down! It's OK. I'm not talking about for long periods, like days or weeks, just a few intentional minutes in the morning to protect your energy.

The first couple of days I did it, it was terrible. Every 10 seconds I had to distract myself from thinking about my phone. *Where's my phone? What messages do I have? Did somebody call? I hope the battery charged. Did I hear it buzz? Dammit, Marie, stop thinking about your phone, it's only 30 minutes.* It's gotten less and less hard over a week, and now I can go a whole hour without it.

The mission, should you choose to accept it, is to learn how to let your big, beautiful brain work itself out. What is on the other side of silence? What is on the other side of boredom when you're not reaching for your phone to fill that void with Facebook, Pinterest, and Candy Crush? There are ideas, creativity, and incredible things inside of that head of yours. If you are willing to give it the space to work itself out and stop filling it and numbing it with your cell phone.

HOW MANY MINUTES COULD YOU COMFORTABLY DETOX FROM YOUR PHONE?

_____

_____

_____

_____

_____

_____

ARE THERE OTHER THINGS YOU COULD DETOX FROM?

_____

_____

_____

_____

_____

WEEK 15

NO MORE ZITS

This week the mantra is "No more zits." I know you're thinking, "WTF are you talking about Marie? What does that even mean?" Let's say you got a big zit right on the tip of your nose. I'm talking a real Bozo looking honker, so big that you've decided to name him Fred, so you can introduce him properly.

The rest of your face is clean and clear, except you can't help but glance at Fred every time you pass a mirror. You touch him several times a day to see if he's growing like a big boy should. You Google DIY remedies for acne in middle-aged women and figure out which concoctions will treat your little problem, and you're definitely making a special trip to the beauty counter for a reload on concealer.

It doesn't matter that the entire rest of your beautiful face is unblemished. The only thing you're going to see is Fred. You're going to focus on the zit non-stop. You're consumed with the zit; you are convinced everyone is talking about it, and you can't believe they haven't invented a zit zapper. You are going to walk, talk, eat, breathe and sleep that zit, even though the rest of your face is beautiful. Why?

What we focus on expands, just like when you're on the market for a new car, and suddenly see that exact car all over town—Law of Attraction. If you are continually thinking about all the inconveniences of life, and the frustrations, that's the zit mindset.

I don't watch the news. It's not because I'm naive, and I want to put my head in the sand, but it's because I know that watching the news does not help my mental health. As an empath, I feel real pain in my body, watching terrible things happen in the world. When I see it on TV, I innately begin to look for it in the world too, I become afraid to even leave my house or let my kids do anything remotely fun. I don't like this feeling; therefore, I choose to see the good. I acknowledge the zit and then intentionally look for something positive to balance the scales.

Pro-Tip: if you don't see anything positive, create it. Random acts of kindness are the kryptonite of negativity.

Life sucks for a lot of people. Many of us end up feeling like there is no hope, but when we can change our perspective from a place of lack and scarcity to a place of abundance and beauty, life is going to transform. Stop focusing on the zits. Start focusing on the things that are good and working for you, because that's what matters.

HOW DID YOU SHIFT YOUR MINDSET THIS WEEK?

_____

_____

_____

_____

_____

_____

WERE THERE ANY INSTANCES WHEN YOU TURNED A NEGATIVE INTO A POSITIVE?

_____

_____

_____

_____

_____

_____

_____

WEEK 16

HAMMERS AND NAILS

Story Time- A father was struggling with helping his son, who was prone to bouts of rage. He was always angry, throwing temper tantrums all through childhood, and by the time he was a teenager, it was starting to get out of control. One day the dad takes him out in the backyard, hands him a box of nails and a hammer, and says, "Every time you get angry, I want you to come out here and hammer a nail into the fence."

The first day he was off to a raging start and had to hammer in ten nails. The second day it was ten nails as well. The third and fourth days, he had nine times when he lost his temper. On the fifth day, he started to see more improvement, only hammering in eight nails. This pattern continued for more than a month. Finally, he got through an entire day without having to hit one nail in.

The young man beams proudly at his dad, "No nails today!" he says. "That's wonderful progress," the dad replies. "Now, I want you to go out into the backyard and pull all the nails out of the fence." The son was confused, but he headed out into the backyard as directed. There are hundreds of nails that he has to pull out of the fence. The nails aren't removed quickly, and the volume of pins is high, so the young man is putting in serious work to get all the nails out as his father requested.

Upon completion, the father says, "This is how your anger impacted my fence, some of those nails you may not even remember hammering in because your rage passed. Just because you don't feel the emotion anymore doesn't mean you didn't leave an impact. Now think about where you left your rage, besides the fence. Who were you mad at, and how did you treat that person? Every time you lash out on the people around you, you are hammering a nail in your relationship. Just like the fence, there will be a hole left long after your feelings pass."

Often, we take our feelings out on people, usually the people closest to us. Whether we're having a bad day, or we're hungry, or they didn't do what we asked them to, whatever the reason is when we're angry, our inner circle becomes easy targets. The anger passes, but it doesn't mean we haven't left a hole in that person's heart. It doesn't mean that that person doesn't have a little wound, and emptiness because of our words and our actions.

In yoga, we learn about something called Ahimsa, which loosely translates to non-violence. On the surface level, non-violence means you don't physically hit somebody, you don't throw things at people, you don't rage externally, but it also applies to your words in the way you treat other people. Mentally, physically and verbally, those are all ways that you can cause harm to somebody. When you finally recover, when you move beyond that emotional situation, you're pulling those nails out, leaving gaps and holes in all of the people you love.

Now we're going to take it a little bit deeper. We're going to talk about the way that we do this to ourselves. All the negative self-talk. The various ways we tell ourselves we're not good enough, smart enough, pretty enough, skinny enough, or tall enough. Every time you do that, you are hammering nails into your *own* fence. Be a steward of your words.

Be a guardian of your thoughts, and quit hammering negative nails into your fence. Remember, just because the thought passed doesn't mean the damage isn't done. It doesn't mean the hole isn't still there. So watch how you treat others and especially watch how you treat yourself.

DID YOU FEEL LIKE YOU REACTED HARSHLY THIS WEEK WITH ANYONE?

_____

_____

_____

_____

_____

_____

_____

HOW DID IT IMPACT YOUR RELATIONSHIP?

_____

_____

_____

_____

_____

_____

WERE YOU ABLE TO REDIRECT YOUR MEAN SELF-TALK INTO A KINDER DIALOGUE?

SEASONAL REFLECTION:
SPRING

Mantra:
If you believe you deserve it the universe will serve it.

Spring brings new life. Plants start resurfacing, and so do your friends. Warmer temperatures give you a chance to finally recharge your Vitamin D reserves, which get depleted in the winter. It's a time of optimism and potential. This is the season we start planting big dreams. It's also a great time to declutter, detox, and organize your life.

Suggested Reading:
- The Path Made Clear- Oprah Winfrey
- Secrets of the Millionaire Mind- T. Harv Ecker

Don't forget to join our on-line family for even more motivational and inspirational content. Search Check up From Your Neck up- Book Club or https://www.facebook.com/groups/413536126011979/

SEASONAL REFLECTION: SPRING

WHAT ARE 3 THINGS YOU WANT TO SOW IN YOUR LIFE?

_____

_____

_____

_____

HOW HAVE PAST SPRINGS IMPACTED ME?

_____

_____

_____

_____

WHAT IS MY MENTAL AND EMOTIONAL STATE IN THIS SEASON?

_____

_____

_____

_____

WEEK 17
EMBRACE THE SMALL STUFF

Story Time- A man was walking on the beach when he sees a woman frantically picking up starfish that had washed ashore and throwing them back into the water. As he got closer, he noticed that there were dozens of starfish stranded in the sand.

He approaches the woman and says, "There are too many, why even bother. You're not going to make a difference." The woman picked up a starfish and threw it into the ocean. She looked at the man and said: "For that one, I made a difference."

You don't have to move mountains to make an impact or win the Nobel Peace Prize to be valuable. By doing nothing, you become a part of the problem. Now imagine if that man had helped her, they would have doubled the amount of starfish being saved. Are you the woman or the man in this scenario? I'm going to guess that because you chose this book, you want to be the woman. You're my kind of people.

Did you know that throughout its life, a bee will only make 1/12 of a teaspoon of honey? That amount is so small you couldn't even sweeten a cup of tea with it, yet a bee never questions its purpose. It still pollinates flowers and contributes to the hive.

This is an interesting fact because we live in a world with billions of people, it can feel like our small voice doesn't matter. We question our worth and devalue our purpose because we don't think our 1/12 of a teaspoon is enough. Now we do nothing instead, forgetting that 1/12 a teaspoon is better than none.

Have you ever heard the buzzing of a single bee? Likely not unless they flew right up to your ear, at which point you probably did the hokey pokey to get it away from you. The sound of one bees' wings flapping is not that loud, but you can hear the hive from several yards away.

That is the power of linking arms with other people who want to make the same impact you do. I am just one voice, but together we can make more noise. One bee only contributes 1/12 of a teaspoon, but a colony can produce 60 to 100 pounds of honey per year, which breaks down to 7,975 teaspoons of honey. I'd say that will sweeten a lot of tea.

Another fun fact about bees, they are not aerodynamically designed to fly. Their body-wing ratio is not supposed to let them. However, they flap those wings with such determination and perseverance they defy gravity. This fact is something I want you to remember when you think you're not built for your dreams.

Nobody said this life would be easy, and flying is certainly not just going to happen by magic. The Wright brothers failed for years at figuring out how to fly, and when they finally did, their first official flight only last 12 seconds, TWELVE seconds of success. They didn't say, "Oh, we can only fly for 12 seconds. It's not even worth it." No. Instead, they kept at it, and as a result, we have plains with beds in them that will fly you to the other side of the globe.

Our mantra this week is to embrace the small stuff. Stop discrediting your contribution because of its size. Look for the small wins. Link arms with others that want to make small changes, and before you know it, you'll be flying.

WHAT IS ONE SMALL THING YOU CAN DO THIS WEEK TO GET CLOSER TO YOUR GOALS?

_____

_____

_____

_____

_____

WHO CAN YOU REACH OUT TO LINK ARMS AND GET EVEN CLOSER?

_____

_____

_____

_____

_____

WEEK 18

NO STRUGGLE NO WINGS

Story Time- A man was taking a walk in nature, and out of the corner of his eye, he saw a little butterfly starting to come out of its cocoon. He sat down and started watching this little butterfly try to break out of the encasing. He sat patiently for over an hour, watching the new butterfly struggle and wiggle. After more time passes, the man realized that the movement had stopped, and it looked like the butterfly got stuck.

He's diligently watching, and still, there's no movement. The man thinks, *"well, good thing I'm here. I'm going to help the butterfly."* So he pulls out his pocket knife and cuts around the edge of the cocoon. The butterfly plops out on the ground. He's all swollen and puffy. When he opens his wings, they not only look frail but short and small.

The man thinks, *"uh oh, maybe he's just got to finish growing. I've never really seen a butterfly come out of its cocoon before."* He scooped up the little guy and took him home to keep an eye on him. Unfortunately, the butterfly was never able to fly and eventually withered up and died.

This story is so compelling because many times in our lives, we are struggling to find our wings. We know it's hard growing and learning how to fly, so we look around for somebody to save us. Somebody to help us out of our tough situation. Somebody to fix us, not realizing that getting that helping hand is going to prevent us from learning how to grow.

Same thing with the butterfly. That butterfly needed to struggle. The only way he can strengthen his wings is by thrashing them against the inside walls of the cocoon. You need that struggle. You need to fight for yourself and quit looking for other people to come and save you or you won't get your wings.

When your parents, spouse, or friends save you from the storm, this help feels good in the immediate situation, but there is a high probability that you're going to get yourself in that same mess. You didn't learn the lesson. You have to figure out how to get through it. And through that struggle, you find your wings.

If it were easy, you wouldn't hold any value over it. Don't look at your struggles as a burden. *Why me? Why do I have these struggles? Why am I going through this mess? Why can't I catch a break?* You're asking the wrong questions.

Every single struggle is helping you be better. So don't look at it as a punishment. Instead see the challenge as a gift. I know that sounds dumb and I know it feels counterintuitive, but it's the truth. There is a lesson in every single struggle. If you spend so much time wishing you didn't have it, you don't get the gift that comes with it. Maybe ask yourself, *why am I facing this again? What do I need to learn? How can I grow from this?*

I've been through a lot of struggles and at the time, they did *not* feel like gifts. Trust me, but now I can look back on the suffering and say *because*

I went through that, I know now I can do this. Challenge yourself this week to push through the struggles. Look at them as an opportunity to find something new inside of yourself. Find your wings. Find the beauty inside of yourself, the strength hiding deep down inside. Discover the power inside of yourself that you didn't know you had before.

HAVE THERE BEEN ANY TIMES IN YOUR LIFE
WHEN SOMEONE HELPED YOU OUT OF A MESS,
AND YOU FOUND YOURSELF IN THE SAME SITUATION LATER?

_____

_____

_____

_____

_____

WHAT IS ONE THING YOU'VE LEARNED ABOUT YOURSELF
WHEN YOU FIXED A PROBLEM ON YOUR OWN?

_____

_____

_____

_____

_____

WEEK 19

I AM NOT MY BODY

Before we jump into this week's mantra, I wanted to tell you guys how thankful I am that you are in my community and how proud I am of you for taking on a bigger role in your life. I see you, boo! Keep going.

I read this quote by C.S. Lewis that says, "You do not have a soul. You are the soul. You have a body."

I think that that is just so incredibly powerful because of how many times we identify wholly with our physical body and we believe that we are the sum of its parts. Things like the color of our skin or how old we are; if we're considered attractive or ugly, tall ,or short; if we have curly hair or straight; the color of our eyes, and my nemesis—weight are only parts of our vessel that we're using to navigate this time here on Earth.

Our soul has nothing to do with that. Who you are inside is what really matters. You are more than your parts. When we identify with our physical body as being who we are, we restrict ourselves by the labels society uses. We open ourselves up for judgment, causing a feeling of less-than to fester in our hearts. Unfortunately, we live in a culture that glorifies physical perfection. So, of course, we naturally look inside and say, *"well, what's wrong with me? I don't have boobs like her, and I don't have a butt like her, and I'm not tall like her."*

These thoughts get played on repeat in our minds until we've depreciated who we are on the inside. Whether your body works perfectly and you're super flexible and strong or you're battling with illness and injuries, I have good news! It is just your vessel. It is not your identity. Give yourself a pass. You are not your body, and you are not the sum of your parts.

How much you weigh, the color of your skin, your height, and the kind of hair that you have do not indicate your level of kindness, your capacity to love, your intelligence, or your generosity. Those are all things that make you who you are, your ability to be kind to people who can do nothing for you, your sense of giving to the world in your charitable contributions to help the people around you. That's what makes you who you are. Not how big you are, not the size of your clothes, not the size of your shoes, not the size of your house, not the type of car you have.

Watch for those pitfalls this week. Pay attention to those feelings of *less-than*, feeling not as pretty, not as valuable, not as smart. Ask yourself, *"am I feeling this way because of my physical appearance?"* Give yourself a pass every time you find yourself in comparison. Nothing's wrong with you because your body is different. You are perfectly beautiful in your imperfections.

WHAT ARE SOME THINGS THAT MAKE YOU UNIQUE,
AND HAVE NOTHING TO DO WITH YOUR PHYSICAL
APPEARANCE?

_____

_____

_____

_____

_____

_____

HOW HAVE YOU LET YOUR APPEARANCE STOP
YOU FROM DOING SOMETHING YOU WANTED?

_____

_____

_____

_____

_____

WEEK 20

SCARS TO YOUR BEAUTIFUL

Have you ever been told to toughen up or get thicker skin? Growing up, I often heard people say, "you've got to toughen up" or "quit being so sensitive." But what does thicker skin even mean and, how do you get thicker skin? What is the thickest kind of skin you can have; well I suppose that would be a scar?

According to the dictionary, a scar is a mark left on the skin or within body tissue where a wound, burn, or sore has not healed completely, and fibrous connective tissue has developed. When you have surgery, the doctor might cut you open and if you have to have that surgery again, the doctor cannot cut through the same spot because that skin becomes so dense, thick, and hard that they can't cut back through it.

So, I want to talk about scars for a little bit because I feel like they get a bad rep. When we've been through some shit in our lives, when we've had to suffer, or made bad choices, we hide it away. We close it off so that the world can't see it because we think that our scars are shameful, for some reason.

When we hide away the darkest parts of ourselves as a secret, it becomes like all other secrets. It grows more powerful the longer we don't talk about it. We walk around feeling like a fraud in our own lives. We think "if they knew what I've been through..." We hold our breath waiting for the other shoe to drop and for someone to announce to the world we are broken.

Hiding away makes getting close to people challenging as well because we've built a fortress around our broken parts. People come into our lives and we assume things like, "she would stop being my friend if she knew I used to be a stripper, he will never marry me if he finds out I had an abortion, they will never respect me if they knew I dropped out of high school." These thoughts loop through our minds until we are convinced we are unlovable because of our mistakes. This week I want to reframe how we look at our painful past.

Your scars are proof that you are victorious in life, that you have made it through some painful things. When we start exposing our truth, we are no longer bound by the dirty dark secret monster hiding under our bed. When we stop rejecting our past, we can move forward into a healthier future. Your scars make you strong. They serve as armor for the terrible things coming your way.

People are motivated by two things— pleasure and pain. When something feels right, we will do it over and over again. When something feels terrible, we will do anything we can to never feel that way again. The thing about scars is that you don't get them without some associated pain. So it makes sense that we don't want to feel those things again This is a catch- 22 because we can actually slowly take the pain away by being open and vulnerable. When we are able to talk about these things, we begin to heal.

Your strength has been forged through your suffering. Own it. That's where you learned how tough you were. That's how you learned what you're capable of withstanding in life, and how to navigate your future. You have to own them like the warrior that you are. Telling my truth not only freed me but also brought people with similar stories into my life. Having someone who went through the same thing you did is also an incredibly helpful part of the healing process. It's precisely why the #meToo movement took off. Women all over the world were coming out of the shadows and saying here are my scars.

WHAT ARE SOME SECRETS YOU'VE BEEN HIDING?

_____

_____

_____

_____

_____

_____

DO YOU KNOW ANYONE THAT HAS BEEN THROUGH SIMILAR THINGS?

_____

_____

_____

_____

_____

_____

WHAT ABOUT YOUR SURVIVAL OF THESE HARD
THINGS COULD INSPIRE OTHERS GOING THROUGH IT?

_____

_____

_____

_____

_____

_____

_____

_____

_____

_____

_____

_____

_____

_____

WEEK 21

CUTTING THOSE STRINGS

Story Time- A reporter was given an opportunity to tour the elephant exhibit at the zoo. She gets invited back to see where the elephants are kept. As she's admiring the elephants, she realizes that they're not in their cages, but instead, they're tied to the cage with a thin string.

When it's time to interview the trainer, she is compelled to ask, "Why aren't these elephants in cages? Aren't you concerned they'll break free from these light strings? Don't they know that they can get away?"

The trainer responds, "No, we're not worried. When they're babies, we shackle them with these heavy chains. Every time they try to break free, they try to buck or get out of their cage, they're yanked back down by the weight of these massive restraints. Over a few months, they learn that when something's tied around their leg, they can't getaway. As they get older, they get used to it being that way. Now, all we have to do is tie them up with this little string. They are programmed to think that string is going to hold them there, and they can't get anywhere."

From very early on, you were chained with ways of thinking. All of the people in your life, parents, teachers, friends, and your family from the time you're born, have been training you to believe what they believe. You have been taught to think a specific way, to believe a certain faith, to love a certain kind of people, that you have to be a certain way to be considered successful.

You are taught these things from such an early age that even after those people are no longer in your life, after you're grown and doing your own thing, you're still bound by that string of belief. These chains convince us we're stuck where we are, that money is hard to come by, that people who believe differently are bound for hell, that it's wrong to love who you love, or that rich people are greedy.

Here's an example. If your mom didn't like onions when you were growing up, and you don't eat onions now, that's possibly a string. That's a chain, a shackle that was placed on you when you were a child because your mother didn't eat them, you are convinced they don't taste good. What an unfortunate string, because hello, onion rings!

That's a very light and airy example but there are lots of examples. Hold your breath, I'm diving in deep — your religious beliefs. Yeah, I went there. Lots of people believe their faith just because it's a family tradition. I'm not bashing religion; I'm asking you to evaluate if you *know* something in your heart to be true because of self-study or if you've blindly accepted it.

Lots of people go into a profession just because their dad did or take over the family moving business to carry on the family name or go to college because they're told it's the only way to get a good job. I want you to examine your life and your beliefs. Look at what is going on and where you feel like you're in a cage. True liberation, true freedom in your life, is when you start cutting those strings, and you start seeing the world through new eyes.

You start seeing new possibilities. You start seeing new ways of living that are far beyond those shackles that you were caged with when you were born. This week we cut those strings. It's time to start taking ownership of your life and stop walking mindlessly through just because somebody told you that's how it was supposed to be. No more blind faith, no more believing because your circle believes.

As you go through your week, notice this pre-programmed packaged way of thinking, the thinking that feels limiting, thoughts that hold you back without having any factual supporting evidence. Those beliefs that bind you and tie you down into the life that you are not destined to live. If you can be courageous enough to cut those strings, you will find a whole new world on the outside of the cage.

WHAT IS SOMETHING YOU LEARNED AS A
CHILD AND HAD A CHANGE OF HEART LATER IN LIFE?

_____

_____

_____

_____

_____

ARE THERE OBVIOUS AREAS OF YOUR LIFE
WHEN PEOPLE HAVE TRIED TO CAGE YOU?

_____

_____

_____

_____

_____

HOW CAN YOU REWRITE THE STORY YOU'VE BEEN TELLING YOURSELF ABOUT YOUR SHACKLES?

WEEK 22

YOU ARE GOING TO DIE.

I know this seems like such a morbid mantra, but I want to remind you because I think sometimes, we forget that life is fleeting. Sometimes we forget that our existence on this planet is very temporary and we walk around as though we've got nine lives to live. That is a fantasy. We wish away days, weeks, and even years of our lives in autopilot, just going through the motions. We spend hours dreaming about the next weekend, holiday, or vacation. Meanwhile hours of each day are vanishing right before our eyes.

How would you live if you knew you were going to be gone tomorrow? Sometimes when people are diagnosed with cancer, their mindset suddenly changes. Imminent death is brought to the forefront of their minds and then they start doing all the things they had been putting off as if having cancer is a pass to live their life the way that they should always have. Trips they always meant to take, books they always wanted to write, and amends with the people they have wronged have now become top of the list priorities.

I'm not blaming them for doing that. What I'm saying is how heartbreaking it is that you have to be diagnosed with cancer to have permission to live your life the way that you always should have. How sad is it that you weren't living up to your potential until you were diagnosed with an illness? Why can't you do that today? Why can't you start doing that right now? No sickness required. No cancer required.

Stop accepting other people's dreams for you. Stop limiting your potential because you're worried about what other people are going to think. You've got one person to live up to, one person whose expectations you have to meet, and that person is you. At the end of your days, when you breathe your last breath, the only person you can blame for not doing the things you dream about doing is you. Yet we spend our days, from sun up to sun down, on the hamster wheel of work, eat, sleep, repeat.

We spend our lives looking to please other people, looking to make sure that we don't rock the boat and making sure that nobody feels like we're taking *too* much. What is "too" much anyway and who even decides that? You deserve as much as you can dream. You have to stop living as if you have unlimited time on this planet. Today choose to do the most with your minutes.

Tomorrow, *if* you wake up, do the most. The next day, do the most. Start living your life like you're supposed to. You are going to die no matter what. Whether you've got six months left on this planet or whether you've got 60 years left on this planet, stop wasting your days. Make the most of each minute.

You are going to die. Stop living your life on autopilot. Stop going through the motions. Decide today to take back your life.

IF YOU DIED TODAY,
WHAT WOULD YOU REGRET NOT DOING?

_____

_____

_____

_____

_____

WHY HAVEN'T YOU DONE THESE THINGS?

_____

_____

_____

_____

_____

_____

WHAT CAN YOU DO THIS WEEK TO MOVE TOWARDS THESE DREAMS?

WEEK 23

YOU ARE NOT STUCK

Some people aren't excited about Mondays, but I am. Monday is a fantastic day, fresh start and clean slate to your week. Regardless of how last week ended, you have a chance to navigate this one on your terms. Even merely choosing this book is a huge testament to your focus and mindset for the days ahead. Serious snaps for you!

Let's talk about the mantra. I want you to remember that you are in charge as you move through your week. No one else has control over your life except for you, and we need to remember this because so many times we've been programmed to think that life is happening *to* us. We accept that we are a product of our environment and have little control over where we are going in life. We feel stuck!

Want to know my #1 secret to transformation? Personal Accountability. You are not stuck with the life that you have. We think it all starts with action. But even before the work takes place, it all begins in your mind with your ownership of your life. You have to find the ability to say to yourself: I do not settle for this life that I've been handed.

Many of you, like me, were given some shit-tasctic cards. I like to equate it to the card game Uno. We start with totally random cards, and along the way, people may make it harder by dishing out a Draw 4 card or Reverse away from your turn. Other times you could have a Wild card that allows you to change the whole game. Either way, you get to decide which cards you play and when. My strategy is to get rid of all the bad cards first, and save all the good cards for last.

Babe, life is not happening to you. You are in charge. You're in the driver's seat. If you are sitting in an experience that you are not happy with, it's time to make some tough choices. It's time to do something different. You can't sit and wallow in the circumstances that you have been born into or handed.

Here are my cards. I lost my father to brain cancer before I turned four, my mother turned to drugs, and within nine months remarried a pedophile, for the next eight years I suffered unspeakable physical, sexual, and verbal abuse. Pile on to that, we lived in OTR (Over-The-Rhine), the worst part of the city prone to riots, gang violence, and drugs. Now sprinkle in being the only white girl. I was a minority among minorities and officially the lowest woman on the totem pole of crap.

If I would have followed in the footsteps of the example that I had been given, if I would have stayed stuck in that poverty mindset in that "woe is me" loop, I would not be where I am. I'm a living testimony that you can change your life. All you have to do is believe that you deserve more and understand that you are in control and then go out there and do the damn thing.

It is easier to settle but your life is going to continue to suck. You have to take ownership of your life. You have to say: "This is mine. I am the only one that has a choice here. I am the only one that can do something to change my circumstances." You are in freaking charge. It's time to start acting like it and take back your life. It is time to take action. That's where it starts. One step at a time. One change at a time. You're not going to get from zero to hero overnight, but you can take one action, maybe one step a day, perhaps one step a week, maybe one step a month. But you have a choice.

If you improve your circumstances by 1 percent each day, you would have a 365 percent improvement a year from now. How would you feel if your life was 365 percent better? I am so passionate about the power that we have at our fingertips, power that we're wasting because we don't realize that we have it. You were born to do more than live a basic life of 9 to 5, pay bills, and die. There is something about you that's special. There is something about you that other people are going to be inspired by, but so many of you are wasting it. Based on my cards, I should not be successful, but I am for one straightforward reason, I believed I could. Now it's your turn.

WHAT KIND OF CARDS WERE
YOU DEALT IN THIS LIFE?

_____

_____

_____

_____

_____

_____

HOW CAN YOU USE THESE CARDS TO GET AHEAD?

_____

_____

_____

_____

_____

WHAT WOULD YOUR LIFE LOOK LIKE WITH 365 PERCENT IMPROVEMENT?

WEEK 24

IT'S OK TO NOT BE OK

Being positive and upbeat is all fun and games until your life explodes. I am struggling this week with a mantra because, well, my life is a total hot mess. My puppy had surgery this week. My basement flooded, and I spent hours shop-vaccing the water up and cementing the whole thing. My kids both had football, so I had to run them back and forth a bunch of times. My husband was out of town, so I had to do it all by myself. Not to mention the cooking, cleaning, laundry, oh, and my three jobs that need my attention.

I have not had a minute to breathe, let alone think about this book. Maybe that *is* the mantra. Perhaps that is what some of you need to hear right now, too. You don't always have to have it together, there I said it. Listen, we're all trying to balance a bunch of things in our lives. The mountain of responsibilities can feel overwhelming, and if you are like me, not getting it done only leads to mom-guilt, self-depreciation, and a deep seeding sense of failure.

We are all juggling a litany of things. I had a mentor, Melanie Huscroft, break it down very simply. We are all juggling two types of balls, some crystal, and some rubber. The crystal balls are precious, if you drop them, they will shatter, and you would be devastated. The rubber balls are also important, but if you were to drop them, they would bounce and you can pick them back up later.

You're going to drop something eventually. We all do. When you load yourself up the way we do, it's inevitable. Nobody is perfect. My crystal balls are my husband, my kids, my dog, *and* myself (working out & taking care of my health). Yes, working out is a crystal ball to me. For a long time, I treated my body like a rubber ball, but friends listen to me- Your health is *not* a negotiable thing! You've only got one body, and if you don't take care of it, you won't be juggling anything. Move yourself to the crystal ball category.

My rubber balls include the laundry, the dishes, and the toilets. I could go on and on about household chores. They're all on the rubber list. Once we have identified the crystal and rubber components in our lives, it becomes easier to navigate the storms that come through.

As you move through your week, remember it is OK, to not be OK. Just hold tight to your crystal balls and give yourself some grace when it comes to everything else.

CRYSTAL BALLS:

_____

_____

_____

_____

_____

_____

RUBBER BALLS:

_____

_____

_____

_____

_____

_____

_____

WEEK 25

IF THE SHOE FITS

Story Time- A woman was completing her training with her guru, and as the end was approaching, she had one final question, "I'm going to go out on my own now. Is it better to dream big or play it safe?" To answer her student, the guru takes her shoe shopping.

The first pair of shoes were beautiful high heeled shoes. As the student stepped into them, she was impressed with how good they felt on her feet, her toes had room to breathe, and it didn't feel like they would create blisters the way many shoes do. She walks around the store feeling supported and powerful in these fancy shoes. She turns to her guru and smiles, "I feel so amazing in these shoes." The teacher replies, "That's wonderful. You should feel amazing in them. They fit you perfectly."

The teacher then requests another pair of shoes for the student. As she begins to put them on, immediately, she notices how small these shoes are. They are so tight she can feel her heartbeat in her toes. The back of her Achilles tendons are cramping, and each step sends shooting pains from the ball of her feet up to her arches. "I don't like these," she grimaces to her teacher. "Let's see how much they cost," the teacher quips back.

The ladies proceed to the checkout counter. "What is the price of these two pairs of heels?" the student asks. "They are the same price," the cashier responds. "The shoes are the same. They're just different sizes."

When we choose to play it safe, you are selecting shoes that are too small. By choosing to dream big you are accepting the shoes that are made for you. As we move through the week ahead notice when it hurts and feels restrictive, pay close attention to what fits. You'll know you're doing the right thing when it fits perfectly. You'll notice you have more confidence. When it is meant for you, it makes you feel like a million bucks.

WHAT FELT RIGHT ABOUT THIS WEEK?

_____

_____

_____

_____

_____

_____

WHAT DIDN'T FIT?

_____

_____

_____

_____

_____

_____

HOW CAN YOU MOVE THE NEEDLE CLOSER TO THE PATH THAT FITS?

_____

_____

_____

_____

_____

_____

_____

_____

_____

_____

_____

_____

_____

_____

WEEK 26

YOU'RE ALLOWED TO SHINE

This past Saturday, I was invited to be one of the guest speakers at a regional training in front of 250-300 ladies. It was wonderful spending time with that many empowered women, but I was slotted to speak second to last. This means I sat anxiously waiting all day. My stomach was in knots by the time I finally got up to speak. Afterward, I was relieved it was over, and thankful I didn't have any major flubs.

Then I decided on my four-hour ride home to watch the playback. It's always dangerous when you watch yourself in playback, because instinctively you go into criticizing mode, or at least I do. First of all, no one likes the sound of their own voice, so you're already cringing. "I don't like how I said that, and I meant to say something else," start looping through my brain. I ask myself questions like, "How do people even listen to me talk?" as I spiral into a fun game of picking Marie apart.

Was it my best effort? No. Was it my worst? Also no. So why am I doing this to myself, I know better. Now writing this book, I have been given a second chance to say the things I wanted to say in my speech before my nerves got the better of me.

One of my talking points was to not be afraid of beast mode. Don't be scared to be the best version of yourself. I started to give a partial snippet of a quote from Marianne Williamson, and now I'm going to write the whole quote for you guys and then share with you what I think about it:

> "Our deepest fear is not that we are inadequate. Our deepest fear is that we are powerful beyond measure. It is our light, not our darkness, that frightens us most. We ask ourselves, who am I to be brilliant, gorgeous, talented, and fabulous, actually, who are you not to be? You are a child of God. You're playing small, does not serve the world. There is nothing enlightened about shrinking so that other people won't feel insecure around you. We are all meant to shine."

> And then she drops bombs later in that passage. "And as we let our light shine, we consciously give others permission to do the same."

I want you to read that quote five more times if you have to because every time I read this quote, it strikes right to my heart. It reminds me that we don't have to play small. We don't have to go into this meek mode. Often, when we're talented at something, we feel somehow compelled to balance the scales and tell everyone how we are bad at something else.

We may say, "Yeah, I'm good at singing, but I can't dance for crap" or "I'm amazing at drawing, but I have dyslexia." What we're doing is not only shorting ourselves of all the power that we have inside of us but we are enabling everyone else to short themselves as well.

I want you to embrace all of the powers that you have inside of you and shine like a frigging star because it is so vital that we start living in our gifts. When I realized I enjoyed public speaking, I hesitated to tell anyone. Should I hate it like others do? Am I conceited? When did we learn that confidence is not OK and that self-deprecation or tearing ourselves down is humility? It's not a form of humility; it is pretend humility if you must tear yourself down to look humble.

Every single one of us has something incredible inside of us. And every single one of us woke up with gifts. I challenge you to live in your gifts and not play yourself down for anyone else's comfort. And I want you to advocate that we all step into our power, and we all permit ourselves to shine.

WHAT TIMES IN YOUR LIFE DID YOU
PRETEND NOT TO BE TALENTED TO SAVE FACE?

_____

_____

_____

_____

_____

HOW COULD YOU HAVE HANDLED THAT
WITHOUT DISRESPECTING YOURSELF?

_____

_____

_____

_____

_____

WEEK 27

WHAT ARE YOU MADE OF?

Story Time- A dad and his college-aged daughter were hanging out in the kitchen. The daughter was expressing her frustrations with her life. She shared with her dad that her boss was unnecessarily critical of her, and her co-workers were cliquey. She went on about how her professor didn't give her the grade that she deserved on a paper. Then on to her boyfriend picking a fight with her and she didn't understand why. She was venting to her father and looking for him to co-sign all of her troubles were not her fault.

As the daughter ranted, her father proceeded to put three pots of water on the stove. In one pot he put an egg, the second he added a potato, and in the last, he poured in coffee grounds. The daughter continued to vent. Her car recently had a flat tire and she made sure he was aware of every frustrating detail that went into repair. On top of the new tire, she had to come up with the money to pay for schoolbooks but was flat broke.

Finally, the father says, "Babe, I have to stop you for a second. Life is like boiling water. Sometimes it'll make you hard like this egg. Sometimes it'll make you soft like this potato. And then other times, the situation will cause you to transform not just yourself, but the water, like these coffee grounds. It all comes down to what you're made of."

Life will always test you. The tests don't make sense right away, the suffering that we're going through feels pointless. No one likes being in hot water. We ask ourselves, why is this happening to me? Then we convince ourselves that nobody has it as hard as we do, and our boiling water is hotter than everyone else's. In all of these situations, there is a lesson. Some teach us to get tougher skin, others to be have compassion, and some teach us how to transform into something new.

None of those lessons can occur without hot water. There had to be suffering for the strength to poke through. I know Forrest Gump said, "life is like a box of chocolates," but I think that is setting us up for disappointment. Life is like boiling water and every time we find ourselves in a hot situation, in a stressful situation, in suffering, there is a transformation that is happening. We have to be willing to peel back the skin and look at what's going on inside.

If we're willing to look at it for what it truly is and stop saying "woe is me." we can find the answers we seek. Next time you find yourself in hot water, start asking what's happening in this situation? Am I getting something out of this? What am I learning? Am I experiencing growing pains? How am I changing? How am I transforming?

You cannot stop the bad stuff from happening, but what you can do is use it, grow from it, and learn from it.

WHAT IS A SITUATION YOU'VE FACED THAT FELT LIKE YOU WERE IN HOT WATER?

_____

_____

_____

_____

_____

_____

_____

HOW DID YOU REACT?

_____

_____

_____

_____

_____

WHAT COULD YOU HAVE DONE DIFFERENTLY?

_____

_____

_____

_____

_____

_____

_____

_____

_____

_____

_____

_____

_____

_____

_____

_____

_____

WEEK 28
JUST SAY HI!

Recently I was on vacation in Mexico with my husband. We'd been there for five days when it hit me that they do something so well there that we don't do back in the States. Every single person at the resorts, the people walking on the streets, and the folks working in the shops try to connect with you. They say "hola, buenos dias," and "buenos noches." Well, they say "noches" and I say "nachos," but they understand and still show kindness even though I'm butchering their language. They actively work to connect with you.

More than merely greeting you verbally, they look you in the eyes! I know, right, eye contact, eek. In our society, we're always on our phones, we're introverted, and we're so locked away in our own worlds that we don't connect with the people around us. We walk down the street, feeling like we're in an isolation bubble. Most of us aren't just alone; we're lonely because of it.

The first day was super challenging because 1. I'm a recovering introvert, and 2. I wasn't expecting any of it; I'm a total deer in headlights at this point. I want to get to my suite as fast as humanly possible. I want to keep my head down, or I want to keep marching, and I certainly didn't want to make eye contact with strangers. By the second day, I realized that this was a thing here and they're clearly not going to stop, so I squeaked out a few holas and didn't die. By the last day, I was a full-blown believer, fully immersed in trying to have, broken at best, conversations, and hi-fiving the staff. By simply saying "hi" to me, the resort made me feel so special and included. Every. Single. Person.

Looking back on that trip, it's not the food or the beach that I miss most. It was being somewhere that people included you. Connection is essential to feeling like we belong. Our society and our humanity depends on feeling involved, in being a part of something. I read a book by Brene Brown, and she says that she thrives on having a strong back, a soft belly, and a wild heart. I absolutely love this.

The problem is, our culture has a strong facade, a weak back, and a fearful heart. And that speaks volumes to our society and why we'd rather keep our head down. Unfortunately, our society also tells us to "fake it till you make it," so we pretend to have a strong façade, and we're afraid of being found out. We pretend to be independent and mimic what we hear from celebrities. Then, compounding the issue, many of us have weak backs, we want it to be easy, and we certainly don't know how to take criticism.

We don't know how to deal with confrontation. Because we're faking our way through life, not connecting with people, and letting other people's opinions hurt us, we end up with a fearful heart. Now, every step that we take, every move that we make is in fear. It's unbearable.

Contrary to popular belief, having a soft belly is not weak; having emotions and being gentle are not shameful characteristics. Having a strong back and a soft belly is healthy balance of vulnerability and power. It means being willing to expose yourself and to say "hi" to people that you don't know.

The more you can connect with the people around you, (your family, friends, and community), the more you are going to feel like you belong on this planet. We need to be seen, to be included in the greater whole. Stop going inside. Stop pretending that you're so strong you don't need to love people, that you don't need to connect with people. This week's mantra is just to say *"hi."*

What if for the next seven days, you said hi to every person you walked by. Say hi to the people in the grocery store, the people at the gas station, the people at your job, the people walking down the street when you're going for a jog, and the people you see while walking your dog. See how it makes you feel inside.

Strong back. Soft belly. Wild Heart.

WHAT ARE SOME OTHER WAYS YOU CAN BE MORE PRO-ACTIVE ABOUT CONNECTING WITH PEOPLE?

_____

_____

_____

_____

_____

WHO ARE SOME PEOPLE YOU WANT TO CONNECT WITH MORE FREQUENTLY?

_____

_____

_____

_____

_____

HOW WOULD IT FEEL TO RECEIVE A KIND WORD OR SMILE FROM A STRANGER?

_____

_____

_____

_____

_____

_____

_____

_____

_____

_____

_____

_____

_____

_____

WEEK 29
JUST SET IT DOWN ALREADY

Story Time- a high school teacher came into her class with a pitcher of water and a glass. After the students were settled, she filled the glass with water and held it out for everyone to view. The teacher asked, "How heavy is this glass of water?" Students shouted out answers ranging from eight ounces to sixteen ounces. When the teacher didn't agree, other students shouted weights in pounds. `

Now the teacher says, "The absolute weight of this glass doesn't matter. It all depends on how long I hold it. If I hold it for a minute or two, it's fairly light. If I hold it for an hour straight, its weight might make my arm ache a little. If I hold it for a day straight, my arm will likely cramp up and feel completely numb and paralyzed, forcing me to drop the glass to the floor. In each case, the weight of the glass doesn't change, but the longer I hold it, the heavier it feels to me."

We've talked a lot about our burdens during this journey, but today I want to give you the biggest piece of advice I could give. Just put it down already. Your stresses and worries in life are very much like that glass of water. Think about them for a while, and nothing happens. Think about them a bit longer, and you begin to ache a little. Think about them all day long, and you will feel completely numb and paralyzed — incapable of doing anything else until you drop them.

Today, I give you permission to set down all of the things you've been carrying for too long. Fears, failures, memories, and relationships set them down. I was given an excellent piece of advice one time: Delete anyone from your phone that makes your stomach hurt when you see their name pop up.

It's not worth your peace, boo. I know it's hard because sometimes it is family but hear me when I say- blood ties do not give someone power in your life. The longer you hold on to them, the more you're going to hurt.

As part of the advanced teacher training at my local yoga studio, we had a burning ceremony. Everyone took the time to write down what they wanted to let go of, then we went outside and set each piece of paper on fire. Lighten your load this week by identifying some things that no longer serve you and visualize setting them on fire.

This is like spring cleaning and incredibly cathartic. When you burn things out, you make space for new ones in your life. You can fill this new part of your life with anything you choose.

Here is an example, say you want to quit drinking. If it's a past time that comes with a particular social circle, you have to cut back on hanging out with those people, even if it sucks. Burn the Friday night happy hours in your mind, and guess what? Now you are free to do something new on Friday nights— Pottery classes, yoga, catch up with a childhood friend; the options are endless.

This mantra is a chance for you to redesign your life in a way that makes you happier. The sky is the limit, but only if you are willing to put some things down.

WHAT IS WEIGHING YOU DOWN?

_____

_____

_____

_____

_____

_____

WHAT CAN YOU REPLACE THE VOID WITH?

_____

_____

_____

_____

_____

_____

_____

SEASONAL REFLECTION:
SUMMER

Mantra:
May all beings be wild and free.

It's time to play! Summer gives us freedom to explore the world, to open our minds to new perspectives, and to grow. Kids are out of school, and many families take vacations this time of year. The heat sets our passions on fire, insights creativity, and energizes our sense of clarity. This season encourages us to test our boundaries, push harder in our efforts, breathe life into our lives. Let yourself fly!

Suggested Reading:
- I Thought It Was Just Me- Brene Brown
- Can't Hurt Me- David Goggins

Don't forget to join our on-line family for even more motivational and inspirational content. Search Check up From Your Neck up- Book Club or https://www.facebook.com/groups/413536126011979/

SEASONAL REFLECTION: SUMMER

PLAN 3 ADVENTURES THIS SEASON:

_____

_____

_____

_____

HOW HAVE PAST SUMMERS IMPACTED ME?

_____

_____

_____

_____

WHAT IS MY MENTAL AND EMOTIONAL STATE IN THIS SEASON?

_____

_____

_____

_____

WEEK 30

THIS IS A TEST

Story Time- It was the end of the school year, and the professor of a local college sent out an email to all the students saying:

Final exams are coming up, but I'm going to give you an option. You can skip final exams and not show up; I will give you a grade on your exam that matches your current GPA. If your grade in my class is seventy-five percent right now, which is a C, then I will give your exam a matching score of seventy-five percent or a C. That will lock your grade in for the semester. Or you can show up and roll the dice and see what life has in store for you.

Test day arrives, and only a few students show up— five or six total. They file into the classroom and take their seats. The professor takes attendance and says to the students: "Thank you for showing up today, you will all receive 100 percent for showing up, and you may leave."

There is a gut check in this story for sure. They didn't even have to take the test? They receive a perfect score just showing up. Trusting and believing in themselves was all it took. What would you have done?

The reason I love this story is because so many of us are settling for half-assed. We are clinging to mediocre mindsets, accepting piss poor salaries and jobs, settling for "less than" relationships with our spouses and friends. Then we're wondering why our lives are so unfulfilling.

Well, babe, it's because you were given several opportunities to excel, but you kept taking the easy route. You kept taking the fast pass instead of doing the scarier thing, putting yourself out there. The harder thing was going in and asking for a raise but because we don't like confrontation, we undercut our value. The good stuff is never attached to an easy path. The best stuff is the hardest to obtain.

You're going to have to exert some blood, sweat, and tears to get it. Nobody gets to the top of the mountain by falling there. You have to climb that shit. It all begins with trusting yourself, believe that you are capable. This is a test; it's all a test. You are always going to be given choices. Some are a little easier, and one's a little scarier. You have to decide what kind of person you want to be.

Do you want to be the kind of person who's always trying new things? Who's always putting themselves out there and manifesting some amazing things? Or do you want to be the kind of person who's just living in the middle? I don't want to be in the middle of the pack. I want to be at the front. I want to be a trendsetter. I want to be creating new things. I want to be forward-thinking. I want to be living my best life.

It reminds me of the scene from Alice in Wonderland. Alice is lost when she meets the Cheshire cat. She asks, "Which way should I go?" and the cat replies, "where do you want to go?" She pauses and then says, "well, I don't know," to which the cat said, "then it doesn't matter what path you take."

If you're not crystal clear about what it is that you want in your life, you will continuously take the wrong path. Once we have clarity around our morals, our integrity, and our goals, we won't be as tempted to take the easy option. This week we are going to choose that harder path, start trusting ourselves and start climbing the mountain.

WHAT AREAS OF YOUR LIFE DO YOU FEEL LIKE YOU'VE SETTLED?

_____

_____

_____

_____

_____

_____

WHAT CAN YOU DO TO CHANGE IT?

_____

_____

_____

_____

_____

WERE THERE ANY TIMES THIS WEEK WHEN YOU CHOSE THE HARDER PATH?

_____

_____

_____

_____

_____

_____

_____

_____

_____

_____

_____

_____

_____

_____

WEEK 31

IT'S TIME FOR A BREAKUP

This week I want to start very vulnerable and very transparent because I am a firm believer that strength is forged in struggle and if we aren't willing to look at ourselves in the mirror, we can't grow. There is a bible verse in Mathew 7:3- *Why do you look at the speck of sawdust in your brother's eye and pay no attention to the plank in your own eye.*

It's easy to look at everybody else and say, so-and-so needs to fix this, and so-and-so needs to fix that. If they just stopped thinking this, then they would be fine. It's very easy to diagnose everyone else and be the neighborhood Dr. Phil. It is super freaking hard to diagnose yourself and to look in the mirror and say, where am I broken? What do I need to fix? How can I get better?

Until you are willing to ask those tough questions, you are going to stay the in same place that you are. You are not going to grow. You are not going to get better, stronger, faster. You are not going to manifest those things that are in your heart, those dreams, those desires until you can start looking within.

I was in Orlando with ten thousand plus of my Younique sisters, and I found myself triggered several times. I was introduced to top leaders, top people in our company whom I admire and respect. I realized something about myself that cut me really deeply. After each encounter with these women of affluence, I walked away feeling like they didn't like me. They probably think I'm a fake. I'm a fraud. I don't deserve to be an Exclusive status in my company, and they know it. This story was on repeat in my brain. I left each one of those meetings feeling like my balloon had been popped, and they could see right through me.

Now, here's the point, I still suffer from self-worth issues even after all the work that I've done. In spite of being somebody that gets on Facebook weekly to inspire, someone who teaches several yoga classes a week to help others, and who speaks publicly, I still have my bad moments. I still have these negative thought patterns that rear their ugly heads because it's a lifetime of unprogramming that I am working through.

It's tough to undo 35 years of bad programming in just a couple of short years. I find myself turning back to my insecurities, leaning back into the person who I used to be with my social anxiety and my introvert tendencies. It's the same story I've been telling myself my whole life. I'm not good enough. I'm not smart enough. I'm not strong enough. They're not going to like me. I am holding my breath because I'm waiting for the other shoe to drop.

Yes, my life started sucky, and I've done something good with it. But deep down inside, I'm waiting for it to be taken away from me. I worry that somebody is going to pull back the curtains, expose the great Oz, and they're going to find out that the whole time I wasn't really deserving, that I must've got in on accident, that it was a mistake.

It's like a radio station. I turned it to that channel, and that's all I was hearing. Thankfully I was able to realize it before the trip was over, I was able to ask myself if it was true. Did they say they didn't like me? Did they tell someone else that? Were they rude or curt with me? What information am I using to create this narrative? Once I looked at it from this angle, I was able to turn the channel and open myself to a more truthful perspective.

Once I flipped the switch, everything changed. I felt like everywhere I turned, someone was asking to take a picture with me, telling me how my story has inspired them, or running up to hug me. I even had some beautiful soul yell from across the escalators, "I love Foodie Friday," (a weekly cooking show I do on Facebook live) to which I yelled back, "I love *you*!"

Bottom line, we need to break up with our stories. We need to break up with those limiting beliefs, those ideas that are solely only in our heads. Do you need a breakup? Is your thought process stopping you from becoming the person you are destined to be? Are you in your own way? Are you your biggest critic? Because it's time to stop that shit. It's time to start drinking your own Kool-Aid, to start believing that you have the power to transform your life.

Start by looking for proof. Ask yourself if it is true, then ask yourself if it is helping you or hurting you. The last question I want you to ask yourself, can I change it? If the answer is "yes," then now you know what you need to do. You need to break up with your limiting beliefs.

You need to break up with that story you're telling yourself that's not serving you. You need to break up with your past. You need to break up with your pain. You need to break up with the people in your life who don't believe in you or support you, and you need to start replacing them with people who do.

Rewrite your story— I'm a survivor, I'm a warrior, and I can get through

anything. I am stronger than my storm. I am worthy of love and success.
I am capable of creating a better life.

WHAT STORY DO YOU NEED TO BREAK UP WITH?

_____

_____

_____

_____

_____

_____

HOW CAN YOU REWRITE YOUR STORY?

_____

_____

_____

_____

_____

_____

WEEK 32

THE BUSINESS OF FISHING

Story Time- A businessman goes on vacation to Greece. While he's on his trip, he's decided to go out for a morning walk and check out the local village. As the man is walking along the shoreline of the little fishing village, he sees a fisherman coming up the shore, and he stops to chat. The businessman is curious about how long he's been fishing. The fisherman says, "Well, just a couple of hours. I caught a few fish."

The businessman is intrigued by this fisherman's life. He asks, "So what are you going to do with the rest of your day?" The fisherman says, "I'm going to handle these three fish I caught. I'm going to sell one to pay my bills. One is to cook and feed my family, and the last one I'm going to give to my friends. Then I'm going to take a nap with my wife. I'm going to play games with my kids in the yard, and eventually, I'm going to go into town, drink wine and play my guitar with my friends."

The businessman says, "Wow, you caught these three fish in just a couple of hours. You know, if you worked a little bit longer, you could catch even more fish. Then if you had more fish, you'd make more profit, and you'd be able to buy a better boat. Once you have a bigger boat, you'll be able to catch more fish. Then you can hire some crew members. After you've got crew members, you're going to be bringing in loads of fish. And before you know it, your profits are going to be so big that you can get a second boat and more crew members, eventually have a whole fleet of ships. It could grow so big that you'll have to move to the city center where you can create a big distribution hub and manage all of your fishing empire."

The businessman is so proud of himself, for being able to help this lowly fisherman with his business. The fisherman replies, "Well, that does sound interesting. How long would that take?" The businessman confidently says, "15, 20 years, tops." "Then what?" the fisherman inquires, and the businessman says, "Well, then I could help you sell your company for millions of dollars and make you very rich." To which the fisherman says, "Yeah. And then what?"

The businessman says, "Then you can move to a small, quaint little village where you can fish when you feel like it. You can take naps with your wife. You can play games with your kids in the yard, and you can drink wine and play your guitar with your friends.

Listen up, friends! There is always going to be somebody telling you how to live your life. Someone who thinks that they know how you should live your life better than you do. They may even be smarter than you. They may make more money than you. They may be older than you and more mature than you. That does not mean that they know the value of your fish.

What we should be working on this week is looking inside, becoming OK with our choices, becoming confident in our gut instinct, moving in a place of knowing what's best for ourselves, and not letting other people tell us how to live our lives. These are your choices, and you have to live with them.

That fisherman could have gone through with that man's plan, and he would have wasted 15 to 20 years of his life to do what he was already doing. Don't waste your life living someone else's dream. Don't let someone else tell you what the value of your fish is. Every choice you make is yours. It's personal. It's special. It's meaningful. The sooner you can tap into that inner voice that's inside of you, your choices are going to be so solid and unwavering, no one's going to be able to distract you from your goals. No one's going to be able to knock you off your path. You're confident, you're focused, you're driven, and you're ready because your choices are rooted deep inside of yourself, not on somebody else's opinion.

Only, you know, the value of your fish.

WHAT DOES YOUR PERFECT DAY LOOK LIKE?

_____

_____

_____

_____

_____

_____

LIST 3 WAYS YOU CAN HELP THIS VISION COME TO FRUITION.

_____

_____

_____

_____

_____

_____

WEEK 33

PEOPLE ARE PRAYING FOR PROBLEMS LIKE YOURS

Friends, these last couple of weeks have been very challenging for me. I've been in a storm. We had to put down our sweet boxer Diesel and my heart is broken. The stress of his illness over the last few months has depleted my reserves and manifested into my physical body. I am sick, and the grief waves keep washing over me. I feel helpless as I watch my children navigate the loss of their best friend and I wish I could take their pain away but I can't. Even as I'm typing this very sentence, I feel a lump in my throat and tears streaming down my eyes.

I like to be transparent because, at some point, your storm will come too and when it does, you could feel like you're drowning. You could be in your storm right now and I want to share the epiphany I had in case it helps. Last night, a bad storm came through our neighborhood and I decided to go out in the garage and watch the rain. It was pouring down hard, thunder crashed loudly, and lightning danced across the sky.

As I sat there with my glass of wine, I was moved by the picture unfolding before me. Amidst the raging storm, I noticed that our lawn had been freshly cut. My husband mowed the grass and it looks beautiful. My mind saw beauty despite the pain. I kept going. We live in a house where the mortgage is paid, without question every month. I have kids who have food in their bellies, and they go to school with clean clothes on their backs. I spend my days teaching yoga and helping women love what they see when they look in the mirror. I was reminded that the storm is not the only thing that matters and that I have weathered far worse. It's tempting to get caught up in the pain of a couple of bad things that are happening and forget how good life is. The mantra that just kept coming to my mind: there are people praying for problems like yours.

People will talk for hours about whether the glass is half full or half empty. But in reality, it doesn't freaking matter. There are two million people that die of dehydration every single year. Whether the glass is half full or the glass is half empty is unimportant. You have a cup, and it has something in it. So drink it and be grateful for your life. Be thankful for your problems because to someone else, those problems would be a relief to the pain they are currently facing.

They wish they had a body like yours because theirs is broken beyond repair. Someone right now is hoping that they find a job like yours with the annoying co-workers you talk about because they have been on unemployment and are at risk of losing their home. Yes, your husband forgot to pick up the milk as you asked him but someone else just found out their husband died, and they would give anything to speak to him one last time.

Don't allow the things that go wrong in your life to steal your joy. It doesn't matter if your glass is half full or half empty. There's goodness in it, something for you to drink. Sometimes you may have to slow down and take a look around, but you will eventually start to see it.

WHAT STORM ARE YOU IN?

_____

_____

_____

_____

_____

_____

_____

WHAT GOODNESS IS IN YOUR CUP?

_____

_____

_____

_____

_____

_____

_____

WEEK 34

CONFIDENCE IS A LEARNED BEHAVIOR

Confidence is a learned behavior. Why do I say that? As a yoga teacher, I often hear things like "I'm not good at yoga because I can't touch my toes, or I won't go to yoga because I'm not flexible." That is the most ass backwards mentality I have ever heard.

How can you ever become flexible unless you start doing the things to make you flexible? So, by saying "I'm not flexible," and then not do something that increases your flexibility, you have just agreed to stay stuck exactly where you are right now in this time, in that inflexible body, stiff and miserable. You're not willing to do anything to improve yourself.

Something magical happens when we start out to do something we are insecure about. At first, it is awkward and very uncomfortable, but the longer we keep at it we start to understand it better. We understand it better and as a result confidence starts to build.

No one is born with confidence. Not a single person is born with self-belief. Some people might be naturally gifted or intelligent, but nobody is naturally confident. We all have insecurities. We all struggle with self-doubt. We all feel like we need approval in the world, but you have to be willing to put yourself out there and see what happens. It's painful. It sucks. You get out there, and you're worried that people are judging you and a lot of times they are. So, you're right. They are judging you. But it's OK. Their judgement is not going to kill you.

The very first time that I spoke publicly on stage, I was in front of 300 women. The only other time I had wanted to throw up more was when I had food poisoning. I get it. It does not feel good to put yourself out on display. But when you put yourself out there, little bit by little bit, you start to build confidence. Now, when you see me getting up on stage, rocking it out, loving every second of it, it's because I kept with it, honed my skill set and now thrive on stage. There was a time it didn't use to be like that, and I had to build that up step by step — painful situation by painful situation. The more you put yourself out there the easier it gets. After the third or fourth time, you'll feel more confident and others will notice it to. This will in turn help validate that improvement and confidence you feel.

It takes time to build any skill. It'll be hard at first but if you're not willing to push through, you're going to be stuck forever. Nobody starts out excellent at anything. You have to practice. And you learn, and you grow. As you try to improve, you turn the painful situations into pleasurable ones where suddenly you're doing that thing that you didn't think that you could ever do. You don't just wake up being able to put your feet behind your head in the yoga practice. You have to show up on the mat every single day. You have to push yourself to your edge frequently and you get closer and closer. As you see progress, you start to build confidence and one day you wake up, and think, *you know what? I can do it*.

Today's the day I want you to make an effort to make this change happen. You're not going to get it on day one or even day five. But by day 50, you'll be glad you pushed through.

Look for the places where you don't feel confident, where you don't feel good enough, strong enough, smart enough and I want you to take a step. I want you to do one thing that freaking terrifies you. Have faith that you're going to start to build some confidence. You're going to begin to build some momentum. You're going to discover new energy in your life that propels you to the place that you want to be, that confident person you want in to be in your life.

WHAT IS SOMETHING YOU HAVE ALWAYS DREAMED OF DOING?

_____

_____

_____

_____

_____

_____

_____

HOW CAN YOU START BUILDING CONFIDENCE IN THIS AREA?

_____

_____

_____

_____

_____

_____

WEEK 35

JADED OR JOYFUL?

I ask that question because it is optional. You get to choose jaded or joyful in this life. Joyful people are not born that way, nor did jaded people come out of the womb with RBF (resting B#$%^ face). Being an optimist or a pessimist is not in your DNA. As a baby, I would wager you were a smiling, cooing, and happy bundle of joy that was only upset when your diaper wasn't changed or when you were hangry AF. The world has impacted you. The struggle can wear you down if you let it.

Have you seen the hand-painted rocks people leave around? Each one is different, when you find one, you're supposed to move them somewhere else. Imagine that you are walking around looking for painted rocks, but days go by, and you don't find any. There are two thought process paths you can take.

The first one: "This is just my luck. No one cares enough to leave rocks in this dumb town. I have some terrible neighbors. They need to get with the program. I should give up. It's pointless to keep looking."

The second path: "I know I've been looking for a while now, so I have to be close to finding one. At least I know where they aren't and that helps me narrow my search. I am going to find one of these rocks."

Now let's apply this same concept to your life. What if you were single but wanted to find a partner? We all know you're going to kiss a lot of frogs, but the jaded mindset will convince you that they are *all* frogs. Everywhere you look you'll see more frogs!

Raise your hand if you've ever had a "friend" talk about you behind your back. Everyone reading this is raising their hand, because we all have, and it cuts deep. Now we have a hard time trusting new friends because we continuously look for them to stab us in the back. We anticipate it, and even worse, sometimes sabotage the good relationships to protect ourselves from getting hurt.

I know firsthand what life can do to a person and I know how it can beat you down. It can make you feel like suffering is all there is. Some people view the world with rose-colored glasses and some with shit colored ones. When wearing the rose-colored glasses, things look optimistic but through the lens of the shit colored glasses, things look pretty shitty.

Have you ever known someone who's so jaded, their negativity spills out onto every single situation? They could be lying on the beach with a margarita in their hand, and they still find the one thing to complain about. They put on the wrong glasses. You could be that jaded, that bitter person, or you can be joyful despite the pain. I choose joy in spite of the hurt. I want happiness, and I don't want to be a miserable cow. That should be the mantra: Don't be a miserable cow.

What if you start to collect your joys like the rock game? Walk around, looking for it. Stop collecting mountains of bitterness and start making piles of joy. Switch the glasses and watch your life change. Be intentional in what you're looking for. You're playing the rock game one way or the other. You're just looking for something different. Choose joy!

WHAT ARE 5 THINGS THAT
BROUGHT YOU JOY THIS WEEK?

_____

_____

_____

_____

_____

DID YOU FIND YOURSELF JADED IN ANY SITUATION?

_____

_____

_____

_____

_____

_____

HOW CAN YOU FLIP
THE SCRIPT ON IT?

WEEK 36
GO INSIDE WHEN IT'S RAINING

Story Time- In an ancient kingdom, the King contracted out all of the artists in the land to paint their version of what they thought peace looked like. There were dozens of submissions of paintings with everyone's idea of what peace symbolized. The King whittled it down to two paintings and let all the people of the town come to view the two finalists.

The first painting was this beautiful landscape, picturesque and serene. There was an image of a crystal-clear lake with snow-capped mountains in the background. The sky was clear and bright blue with just a couple of fluffy clouds floating in it. All the people in the land agreed that this was the picture of peace.

The second painting was a similar landscape picture, but it was not quite so serene. The water in the lake was very turbulent. Next to the lake was also a mountain, but it had a big waterfall crashing into the lake, making the water very tumultuous. The cliffs were jagged. The sky was dark gray and cloudy, and it looked like a terrible storm was about to erupt. The people were confused as to why this painting was being considered. It didn't look very peaceful at all.

The King looked at that painting and pointed out to the viewers something they may have overlooked. Near the edge of the waterfall grew a bush, and on that bush, the artist painted a sleeping robin in nest. The people gathered around for a closer look.

After allowing them to ponder for a few minutes, the King announces that the second painting is the winner. This dark and gloomy painting is a more accurate representation of peace because peace is not found when conditions are perfect. Peace is not found when everything is lovely and serene. We cultivate inner peace in the middle of the storm, when things are chaotic, when things are stressful and out of your control.

Real peace generates from inside, it's not something that we can find externally. It's something that's already in us, and we have to tap into it. But we're so busy thinking, "oh, if I could just lose 10 pounds, I'd be happy" or "if I just made a little bit more money, I wouldn't be so stressed." So we slave away trying to fix what's going on around us.

We get lost looking for it somewhere else, trying to change our circumstances with the idea that our happiness has to fit in a pretty little painting. When it doesn't align with our ideas it frustrates us even further. Suffering occurs when our expectations don't align with reality, we expect things to go smoothly, and when they don't, it spins us for a loop.

Have you ever known someone that was always in panic mode? Even the slightest challenge put them into a spiral. They stress about even the smallest hiccup to the plan. Is that person you? Here's the thing about pressing the panic button: you stop thinking clearly, you let your emotions take over, and as a result make resolution even harder to accomplish. You can be in the worst storm but if your mind is clear, you can be calm, cool, and collected.

I think it is one of the reasons why some athletes and celebrities struggle with drugs. For most of their lives, they told themselves that their life would be different when they made it. When they hit this goal or get that contract all their problems will magically go away. Then they make it and realize the dream they chased for so long was not the key to their happiness. It's like having the rug pulled from underneath you.

It is the same reason why we are told to let our babies cry. If we are always jumping in every time they cry, they aren't going to learn how to self-sooth. They cry for a while but eventually adjust to their environment. They learn it is ok to be alone, and that's what we sometimes forget how to do as adults.

I'm OK if it works out the way I want it to, *And* I'm OK if it doesn't. As you move through your week, I challenge you to be quiet in the storm. Visualize yourself as the sleeping robin in the second painting. Allow yourself to be ok with what's going on around you and not attach to the results or expectations of the stressful situation. That's what real peace is. Just go inside when it's raining and sooth yourself.

WHAT STORMS CAME THROUGH THIS WEEK?

_____

_____

_____

_____

_____

_____

_____

HOW DID YOU NAVIGATE THEM?

_____

_____

_____

_____

_____

_____

WERE YOU ABLE TO GO INSIDE TO CALM YOURSELF?

_____

_____

_____

_____

_____

_____

_____

_____

_____

_____

_____

_____

_____

_____

WEEK 37

DON'T TELL YOUR BIG DREAMS TO SMALL-MINDED PEOPLE

L et's daydream for a minute and go back in time to when we were little, right around six or seven years old. What did little "you" want to be when you grew up? How did you view the world?

I wanted to bring this back to the forefront of your mind because when you were a child, you likely had big dreams. Little Marie wanted to be a psychiatrist, and I boldly announced it to my second-grade class. Looking back, I realize the reason I wanted to be one is because, until that point, psychiatrists were one of the kindest people I had met. They tried to help me, I always wanted to help people like me, so being one felt like the right choice, but I digress.

Kids have an incredible ability to color outside the lines, to dream big and make bold statements. They have no idea what they aren't capable of according to society's standards. That's why when you ask a 7-year-old what they want to be when they grow up, they say things like the

President, an astronaut, or Superman.

No dream feels off-limits. My kid wants to drive a Bugatti and be a millionaire off of YouTube videos. He shares with me what his gaming room will look like and what kind of "merch" he will create for his followers. Real talk for a moment, I had to catch myself, even being the enlightened, entrepreneurial unicorn I am, the mother in me wanted to redirect his dream to something more "reasonable."

That is exactly what happens to most of us. Throughout our childhood, one by one, grown-ups have told us to shoot a little bit lower. Play a little bit smaller, until it feels like all of society is telling us to scale back our expectations. Usually, it's our inner circle, the people who care about us and want to protect us. And they give us fear-based advice because they care.

You have to be careful of those nay-sayers, and I will tell you guys that they will come disguised as people who care about you. It will be your family and your friends. It will be your cousins, your aunties, and your uncles. They are all going to think that they're giving you good advice. But really what they're doing is limiting your potential. They are asking you to play small sometimes for their own comfort, sometimes from their own experiences and sometimes to protect you.

Let me tell you this right now—you will never be everything that you are designed to be in this world if you are continually playing small with those people. You have to be willing to cut ties with anyone who doesn't believe in your potential. Cutting relationships is hard. Trust me, I've had to protect my dreams, too. Just remember, you are the sum of the five people you hang out with.

If you are trying to change your life and your five people who you hang out with are broke, guess what? You're going to be the sixth broke person. If you are trying to quit smoking and your five best friends all smoke, guess what? It ain't happening. You can't make changes under these conditions. You can't become the person you are designed to be and still stay precisely where you are right now. Now imagine you started hanging out with five millionaires instead of five broke friends, guess what? Odds are you're going to be the sixth millionaire. You hang out with chickens, you fly like a chicken but if you hang out with an eagle you learn to fly like an eagle. Stop giving other people power over your life.

You have to be conscientious enough to realize that not everyone cares about your success the way you do. It is only your job to get you where you need to go. You don't require anyone's approval. You don't need anyone's validation, and if you are looking for somebody to cosign your dreams, sit with me. Just as I did with my son, I will cheer for you too.

We recently had a vision board party at my house this weekend with a bunch of ladies, and I loved it. They were asked to dream big, but one thing I noticed was that each one of them was dreaming just a little bit small still. It didn't matter that this was a vision boarding event, and we were envisioning our BEST version of ourselves, they were all again playing small. You know why? Because society has programmed us to play it safe.

This week the mantra is straightforward: Don't tell your big dreams to small-minded people. Become a guardian of your dreams, protect them like gold, and only share them with people who you can trust to support you. Pay close attention to their responses, and make a mental note to stop sharing with anyone that gives you the guidance to be "reasonable."

Become a steward of your inner circle and start swapping out small fish for big fish. This life is a big pond baby and if you're looking for people to link arms with, if you want to surround yourself with people who believe in destiny, and the power of your potential you're welcome to

join our online community. We have a Facebook group titled the same as this book. You can join if you haven't done so already.
Search Check up From Your Neck up- Book Club or https://www.facebook.com/groups/413536126011979/

Remember these are your dreams and they were given to you for a reason. Get out there and manifest them. No more waiting for somebody else to permit you to live your best life. You are designed for greatness. You wouldn't be here living, breathing, existing if there wasn't more for you to give in this world.

WHAT DID LITTLE 'YOU' DREAM OF BEING,
AND WHAT STORIES WERE YOU TOLD
ABOUT BECOMING THAT?

_____

_____

_____

_____

_____

WHO IN YOUR CIRCLE IS A NEGATIVE NELLY,
AND HOW DOES THAT IMPACT YOUR GOALS?

_____

_____

_____

_____

_____

WEEK 38

TIME MANAGEMENT IS A MYTH

Why did I write this book? I've asked myself that question at least 100 times. Here's the deal, I noticed a trend in people I've met throughout the last few years, a reoccurring theme of discontent in their lives, and I wanted to help. I know I don't have all the answers, but we grow by sharing, so I'm sharing in hopes that there is something I've learned that could help you.

I think it's vital that we set ourselves up with an intention for the week, that we're not just mindlessly wandering and meandering through our days. That's kind of what I wanted to home in on this week — the idea of time management. If you are the kind of person who says things like "I just don't have enough time in the day" or, " I just need better time management skills" I'm dropping a bomb this week.

Those things are *not* your problem. We don't need better time management. It is impossible to manage your time. Oh, you think it is? Then try stopping time right now. Go ahead. Try to stop the clock. If you could manage time, then that means you have the power to stop and start at your will. Fast forward or rewind time. Nope, we don't have that ability.

Side bar- *Click* was a great movie about a guy who had the power to control time, if you haven't seen it or it has been a while, I recommend that you watch it this week.

Do you have the power to make more time, or assign time to someone? Also, a big fat no! That clock keeps on ticking whether we like it or not. What we can manage is our priorities. Everyone starts with the same 24 hours in a day. There is a cute meme that floats around, and it says- "You have the same amount of hours in a day as Beyonce." <insert mic drop here>

Some people are just prioritizing their time differently to make it more effective. The life that you have right now is a direct result of how you are choosing to use your 24 hours. If you're broke, it might be because you're not using any time on a side hustle. If you're unhealthy and overweight, it might be because you're not using any time to invest in going to the gym and working out or meal prepping. How you use your time is a direct reflection of the quality of life that you have right now. So if you want a better quality of life, choose to use your time differently.

I can hear you already: "Marie, you don't understand. I work a full-time job and have kids." Let's say you wanted to get out of debt, but you're not sure how you could fit it in a second stream of income. The first thing you need to do is become crystal clear on what you are spending your time on. Think of it as a time diary. Here is a reasonable breakdown:

Work	8
Commute	1
Chores/Cooking	1
Dinner	0.5
Homework	1
Hygiene & Personal Care	1
Workout	0.5
Sleep	8 (uber generous, highly productive people sleep less)
Total	**21 hours**

That is three hours of unaccounted time. What do you imagine is happening during this time? 180 minutes wasted unless you assign it! That is the key.

You want to go back to school, take an online course, you have three extra hours. You want to start a side hustle creating homemade candles made of bees' wax? I bet you could do some serious damage to your business task list in three hours. You want to write a book? I wrote this book in one-hour chunks. Three hours a day, seven days a week for a whole year, and you will have dedicated 1,095 hours to your passion project.

What we really need is priority management. From now on, instead of saying, "I don't have time for something," try saying "It's not a priority." Let's try it on.

Instead of saying, "I don't have time to work a side business," say "financial freedom isn't a priority" and notice how it changes what you feel it inside. Notice how you might suddenly start to make it a priority.

There is power in assigning your time. If you have a vision, dreams, and aspirations, it has to become a priority. You have to be disciplined enough to say "I have places to be and things to accomplish. I cannot spend my time Netflix and chilling. I cannot spend my time hanging out at the bars, getting wasted every weekend. I cannot not spend my time hanging out with people who don't want to grow."

You have the same amount of time as Beyoncé, and I would wager she isn't sleeping eight hours a night. Time is the only thing more valuable than money, and we are wasting it. I wear a lot of hats—mom, wifey, yoga teacher, program manager, podcast producer, makeup mogul, and now author— and I don't get it all done by magic. I get it all done by being focused and knowing that one day my time will run out. The saddest thing to me would be to die knowing I didn't live up to my potential.

WHAT DOES YOUR TIME AUDIT LOOK LIKE?

_____

_____

_____

_____

_____

HOW CAN YOU BETTER PRIORITIZE YOUR TIME?

_____

_____

_____

_____

_____

_____

WHAT ARE SOME SACRIFICES YOU
COULD MAKE TO GET CLOSER TO YOUR GOALS?

WEEK 39

WHAT KIND OF PALACE ARE YOU BUILDING?

Story Time- In an ancient village located at the foothills of the Himalayan mountains, there lived a man who was considered a master builder. He was well known throughout the land for his impeccable attention to detail, and his craftsmanship was unparalleled. People would come from other villages to admire the palaces he built.

The master-builder served the king for decades. The king became ill and died from complications, so his son took over as the ruler of the land. As he was getting on in years and starting to feel the burden of construction weighing down on his body, the master-builder went to the young king to request his retirement.

"Of course!" said the new king, after he listened to the master-builder, explain why he was ready to retire. "I have one last request, can you build one final palace? Then you can take your retirement in peace." The master-builder stood there stunned, he knew he could not refuse, but he did not want to build anymore. He begrudgingly agreed and left the king to set about planning.

As plans were developed, the master-builder felt resentment building. *"How dare this young king ask me to build another palace? Doesn't he realize I served his father for years? I have created dozens of palaces for his family; why does he need another?"* He thought to himself.

Construction ensued, and the master-builder could not shake this increasing animosity. He wanted to get this palace done as quickly as possible, so he made it smaller than all his others. Instead of two wings, he downsized it to one. He chose cheaper building materials because they were easier to get, and he even started stealing from the building fund. He told himself he had earned every penny he stole, and it was a small price considering how the young king offended him.

Finally, the palace was ready. The king assembled the whole town, including the master-builder and his family. The young king stood on the steps in front of his people and said, "Master-builder, you have served my family for years. Your contribution to the community cannot be matched, but I would like to gift you this palace as a token of appreciation for all your hard work."

This week the mantra is going to punch you right in the face. We all know what it is like to feel undervalued, under-appreciated, and underpaid, but it is who we are when no one is looking that defines our character.

Does other people's inability to see your worth give you a pass from doing the right thing? When your boss leaves for the day do you check out too, while staying on the clock? Are you doing the bare minimum to say you got it done?

Integrity is one of the few things that we cannot afford to bargain with. Doing the right thing even if you don't get a reward for it, even if no one sees is true integrity. By bartering that away out of resentment, you are unintentionally building a crappy palace that you have to live in.

Now you're paranoid, looking over your shoulder. You can't even enjoy the good fruits of your labor because deep down inside you know you have been cutting corners. You know you could be doing better but you aren't. Shame builds, and now you're drinking a delightful cocktail of insecurities and secrets, the kind of shit that keeps you up at night. This is *not* the house you want to live in!

There is something very satisfying about laying your head down at night, knowing you did your best. Even if you didn't get a trophy, you know in your heart it was the right thing. You can sleep better with a clear conscience.

In the words of the wise old sage, Jiminy Cricket, "If you repeat a lie long enough, it becomes the truth." You get to the end of your days and look back to realize you built your palace with lies, trickery, laziness, and weak moral character.

Good news! It's a new week, and that means a chance to do better. Just because you have done it in the past doesn't mean you have to keep doing it. You get to decide right here and know what kind of palace you are building, with your actions and your commitment to doing your best no matter who cheers for you.

HOW ARE YOU CUTTING CORNERS?

_____

_____

_____

_____

_____

_____

_____

WHY?

_____

_____

_____

_____

_____

_____

_____

WEEK 40
REPLAY THE GOOD

heard a quote this week, author unknown, it said, *you can't laugh at the same joke twice, so why do you cry over the same pain twice?* That registered deep down into my bones because when things hurt us, they really hurt. As I've gotten older, though, I have realized, joy and suffering are two sides to the same coin. For some reason, we end up just focusing on one side of the coin. That's all we see, and we get into this vicious replay.

It's like a nightmare loop of all of the bad things that have ever happened to us. We lay down in bed in bed at night and think, "oh, I haven't thought of this awful thing in a while, let me relive it." When was the last time you replayed a happy memory?

Instead, you choose to go back to that ugly memory. You let yourself go back and reopen that wound. Yes, I said it, you choose. Long after the situation is over, and the worst of it has passed, we inflict *more* pain on ourselves again by going back to that memory. You can't laugh at the same joke twice. Why do you cry over the same pain twice?

We are the master of our own suffering because we are the perpetrator this time. Think about this: When was the last time you laid in bed thinking about the day you gave birth to your child? What it felt like to have them in your arms for the very first time and what it felt like to watch them learn to crawl, take their first steps, and said your name for the first time.

What did it feel like on your wedding day? How did you feel as you saw your future spouse? How about the reception? Did you dance, when was the last time you listened to your first dance song? These are the memories that should be replayed; don't you agree?

When was the last time you thought about that breathtaking sunset you enjoyed on your last vacation? Or thought about the sense of pride you had when you bought your first home? How about high school or college graduation? So many good memories you forgot about, right?

There are so many amazing memories that you could relive, but you choose to go back to the negative ones. So this week, my challenge to you is to replay the good. Don't live in the negative. Don't go back to the painful memories; go back to some good memories instead.

If you don't have any good memories, which is hard for me to believe, but for argument's sake- you don't have a good memory, imagine a good memory. Imagine the life that you want, a beautiful life filled with all the incredible things you wish you could have.

This is a concept I call dream building. At night before you fall asleep, you play out happy scenarios, planting seeds into your subconscious mind of the life you want. Start manifesting good things by thinking about them right before you fall asleep.

I'm not saying pretend it didn't happen; I am asking you not to let the past keep a hold of your future. Memories, in general, are like a chain reaction. One lousy memory reminds you of another, and you spin your wheels for hours in pain. The same goes for good memories.

Like I was saying earlier, the first good memory may be the time you held your baby in your arms for the first time. Then suddenly, you start to remember them playing with their toys, or playing with your family pet. Now you're on a roll, and you remember celebrating when they said their ABC's for the first time or said "I love you" with slobbery kisses. Those are the beautiful parts of your life.

If you're going to let your mind go nuts and live in past memories, let it be something good. Let it be something that's going to make you feel happy in your life. You get to choose.

LIST 3 OF YOUR HAPPIEST MEMORIES THAT YOU WANT TO LIVE IN WHEN THE PAST CREEPS IN:

WEEK 41

KINTSUGI

Have you ever heard of Kintsugi? No, it's not a sushi roll. It's an ancient Japanese tradition where they take broken pottery mugs, bowls, plates, and they put them back together with liquid gold. The idea is that- just because something is broken doesn't mean it can't be useful anymore.

Once we can learn how to put it back together, it becomes more valuable, it becomes more beautiful, and it becomes stronger. Did you hear me? I'll say it again for the people in the back. After you put the pieces back together, it becomes stronger, more valuable, and more beautiful.

A yoga teacher once told me, "Everyone comes to the mat broken. Some are broken in their bodies, some in their minds, and some are broken in their hearts." As I've grown, I have realized this doesn't just apply to yoga. We all know what it feels like to be broken.

I learned about Kintsugi while I was in Utah at the Haven Retreat, a place for survivors of child sexual abuse, to go and find hope and healing.

While I was there, we created a piece of Kintsugi in symbolism for the work we had to do as survivors in healing. Before we could begin, we had to take a hammer and smash a perfectly good bowl into pieces. This hit my heart as hard as it hit my bowl.

If you don't take the hit, you have nothing to put back together. So many times, I had wished I didn't have to go through all the trauma. I frequently thought why did this happen to me? But at that moment, I realized that taking the hit is what taught me how much I could bear. That life could throw the worst at me and I could put the pieces back together.

Another interesting thing I noticed doing this activity was how long you had to sit and hold one piece for it to set in place. I am not pre-disposed to be a patient person, so this was particularly challenging for me. I'm a Taurus and I know I can be stubborn and want things on my terms.

Healing cannot be rushed. It takes time and patience. When I tried to let go too soon, the piece would fall off, and I would have to start all over again on it. I learned to give myself some grace, to be okay with my broken parts.

One problem that exacerbates the issue is that we're all spending too much time on Facebook trying to pretend like we're not broken. We filter out our scars. We pretend perfection which doesn't help you address your issues. And it certainly doesn't help the viewer who feels like they are the only ones going through it, suffering in silence. It's one of the reasons I love the #meToo movement. It encourages women to speak up and creates a sisterhood of healing.

If I survived it and you're going through it, shouldn't I explain to you how I did it? Shouldn't I show you how to put the pieces back together? Why are we trying to pretend like we're perfect? Our brokenness is what makes us beautiful. Be the hand that reaches back to pull others up.

You have proven that you can get through these awful things. You did the hard part of putting your life back together. You have determined that you can take a hit, and now you're stronger, more valuable, and more beautiful. Shine on, my friend!

If you are a survivor or know a one and would like information about the retreat, please visit: www.youniquefoundation.org

WHAT KIND OF HITS HAVE
YOU TAKEN IN YOUR LIFE?

_____

_____

_____

_____

_____

_____

ARE THERE THINGS THAT HELPED YOU
PUT THE PIECES BACK TOGETHER?

_____

_____

_____

_____

_____

WHAT DID YOU LEARN ABOUT YOURSELF ALONG THE WAY?

_____

_____

_____

_____

_____

_____

_____

_____

_____

_____

_____

_____

_____

_____

_____

_____

SEASONAL REFLECTION:
FALL

Mantra:
You must participate relentlessly in
the manifestation of your blessings.

Fall is all about abundance, harvesting the things in your life that you have been growing. In harvest there is always work to be done but the bounty is plentiful. The leaves are changing colors and the temperatures begin to cool showering us in the beauty of transition. There's also football, firepits, and s'mores. This season creates space to recount your blessings, and to offer generosity to those less fortunate.

Suggested Reading:
- Atomic Habits- James Clear
- Year of Yes- Shonda Rhimes

Don't forget to join our on-line family for even more motivational and inspirational content. Search Check up From Your Neck up- Book Club or https://www.facebook.com/groups/413536126011979/

SEASONAL REFLECTION: FALL

LIST 3 WAYS YOU CAN PAY IT FORWARD:

_____

_____

_____

_____

HOW HAVE PAST AUTUMNS IMPACTED ME?

_____

_____

_____

_____

WHAT IS MY MENTAL AND EMOTIONAL STATE IN THIS SEASON?

_____

_____

_____

_____

WEEK 42

ASK AND YOU SHALL RECEIVE

If you don't ask, the answer is going to be no. So many people are unhappy with their lives and want more, but they're afraid to ask for it. Then they sit and stew, about how they have nothing and often become bitter as a result. That's how the universe works; you have to be brave enough to say: I want more from my life.

You have to be willing to at least ask for more, or else you are not going to it. You have to be brave enough and strong enough to raise your hand and say: I want more financial stability, I want more quality relationships, I want more education, I want more job security. Ask for it. Put it out there. Talk to people about it. They may be the one that unlocks your blessing, but if they don't know you want it, they can't help you get it.

Stop putting the keys to your desires in other's hands. If you're sitting back waiting for somebody to give you something, hoping to win the lottery, or for some Prince Charming to come along and pluck you up out of your circumstances, it isn't going to happen, Booboo. You have to ask for the things that you want. You can't sit around waiting to be saved. You have to take your life into your own hands, and it starts with telling people what you want.

If you don't like the way people are treating you, then you ask them to treat you differently. Don't bite your tongue and allow them to treat you that way. That's just going to create more misery and discontent. True suffering comes when your expectations don't align with your reality.

For this suffering to stop, you have to change your reality to match your expectations. You cannot do that if you're not willing to ask for things to be different. You have to say, I want this and stand firm in that. I want a man who supports me. I want a man who brings me coffee in the morning. I want children who do their homework when there's homework to do. (I'm still asking for that last one, but I'm working on it).

I want to be happy with my job. I want to make more money. These are all things that you have to ask for. You cannot sit around, hoping for it. You want a promotion at your job? You will be waiting a long time if you think that your supervisor will wake-up one morning with your promotion on their brain. Are you secretly waiting for your supervisor to walk in and wave a magic wand and bippity, boppity, boo you to the next level? People cannot read your mind. Tell them that you want that promotion. Be brave and put your name in the hat. You have to show up every day to get that promotion. You can't just hope that somebody is going to say, "You know who deserves this? She's been working in silence for five years. She's the one that deserves this promotion." Nope! They're not going to notice unless you ask!

If you want something, go out there and take it. Go out there and put it to the universe and say, I want this. Keep in mind that you still might get a "no," but it's the only way that you might get a "yes." If you don't ask, you're absolutely getting a no but if you're willing to put it out there, if you're ready to put yourself on the line a little bit, you could get a yes.

That's where the victory happens. That's where the change happens. You're not going to get it if you're sitting around waiting for somebody to save you, waiting for somebody to fix your life, waiting for somebody to come bail you out, or waiting for that lottery ticket. Go out there this week and take charge. Get in the driver's seat of your life.

WHAT IS SOMETHING YOU'VE BEEN HOPING FOR?

_____

_____

_____

_____

_____

_____

_____

HOW CAN YOU PUT IT OUT INTO THE UNIVERSE?

_____

_____

_____

_____

_____

_____

_____

WEEK 43

SPEAK LIFE

Did you know you have a superpower? That is right; you were born with it. We all have it, and oftentimes we take it for granted. Your power is the power of words. We have the power to either build someone up or tear someone down with one fell swoop.

We have the power to speak life and give someone a little bit of confidence, motivation, and support. Likewise, we can send them spiraling into anxiety, self-doubt, and insecurities in a matter of minutes.

The world can be a sucky place. Every single person you come in contact with is fighting a battle that you know nothing about. They will not remember what you gave them, but they will remember how you made them feel. What if you were the one bright spot in their day?

So as you move through your week, friends, I want you to determine if you are speaking life into those around you or if you are speaking death. Elevate yourself by elevating your words and the way that you speak to other people. People will be drawn to you.

Let them know that you're in their corner and then when you need it, guess who's going to be there? All those people who you poured into, encouraged, and cheered for. Be the calm voice through their dark storm. Guess what happens when you're going through your storm? They're going to come out in droves. They're going to stand by you and link arms with you. You're going to realize that you built an army of people willing to cheer for you because you started it.

Be the change and lead by example. Everywhere you go, speak life into people. You see that mom, that single mom struggling? Give her some words of encouragement. You see that older woman going back to school and she's a little bit nervous about it? Cheer her on and let her know that she's capable of beautiful and amazing things in her life. You see that dad trying to help his daughter with her dance recital and fumbling over his feet? Remind him of how important it is for him to do this for his daughter.

As you go through your week, just say "no" to being an internet troll with keyboard courage. Say "no" to gossiping about your co-worker's new outfit. Resist the temptation to fall back into old thought patterns of negativity. Be a light and speak life.

WHAT IS THE BEST COMPLIMENT
YOU EVER RECEIVED?

_____

_____

_____

_____

_____

_____

WHAT IS AN INSULT THAT STILL STINGS
WHEN YOU THINK ABOUT IT?

_____

_____

_____

_____

_____

WHEN WAS THE LAST TIME YOU FOUND
YOURSELF GOSSIPING, AND HOW CAN
YOU PROTECT YOURSELF NEXT TIME?

_____

_____

_____

_____

_____

_____

WHO DID YOU UPLIFT THIS WEEK?

_____

_____

_____

_____

_____

WEEK 44

WHITE SPACE MATTERS

Story Time- It was the first day of school, and the professor stood at the front of the class while all the students filed in and took their seats. After everybody was sitting down, he proclaimed that they were going to have a pop quiz. All the students looked at each other, confused because it's the first day of school. *"How are we going to have a pop quiz? We haven't learned anything yet,"* they murmured. The professor just reassured them that he might not grade this, but he wants them to be open-minded.

He hands out papers to all the students face down. Everybody is still really concerned because they don't know what to expect. They haven't learned anything yet and this is an odd request for the first day of school. The professor cooed, "It's just a test. All I want you to do is write what you see when you turn the paper over."

On the professor's queue, the students turn the paper over. Now, confusion rates are skyrocketing, as they notice that there's only one tiny black dot at the center of paper. Thinking it's a misprint, they start looking over to see what the folks have on theirs. It's all the same white piece of paper with a black dot on it. The professor urges them again, "Just write about what you see."

Ten minutes pass, and the professor collects all of the papers. He stands at the front of the room and reads out the answers one by one. Each student described the little black dot a little differently. Some students described how big it was in circumference and others commented on the intensity of the black ink. After he read every single description, the professor put down the papers and said, "If I were to grade this, you would all get a 50 percent, because all you did was describe the black dot. None of you explained the whitespace."

When we have dark spots in our lives, they have a way of taking over. They feel more significant than they are and often convince us that they're the only things we have. When we have things that frustrate us, that make us angry, that get on our nerves, somehow, we get tunnel vision, and all we think about is how annoying that one thing is. It takes over everything. We start seeing nothing but the black dot, which is only one percent. Your life is ninety-nine percent good, that's the white space.

There is something I learned about a few years ago called the Rule of 5. If it won't matter in 5 months, don't stress about it for more than 5 minutes. That will free you from spending more time on the negative and focus more on your goodness.

WHAT ANNOYED YOU THIS WEEK?

_____

_____

_____

_____

_____

_____

_____

HOW LONG DID YOU LET IT BOTHER YOU?

_____

_____

_____

_____

_____

_____

_____

WHAT CAN YOU DO TO CUT
THAT TIME DOWN, MOVING FORWARD?

WEEK 45

KINDNESS IS THE KEY

Recently I flew to Vegas for a female entrepreneur training, I like to attend as many events as I can because I want to be a sponge to this world. This event left me on a big high. These women are inspiring and motivating. There was one particular moment that is still lingering on my heart. One of the speakers said that she thought her only job in life was to collect smiles.

I've been chewing on this one for a while. How do we start to collect smiles? Not only that, I am inspired to share this idea with my children. Can we become smile collectors in our life too?

I was talking to my son last night on the way to dinner, "What if I asked you to make five people smile today?" I started. He thinks for a moment and says, "that would be really hard mom." I asked him why he thought that, and he didn't have an answer. We arrived at the restaurant and were seated at our table. The server approaches and takes our drink order. I looked at her and said, "I really like your makeup." She smiled, thanked me and walked away.

"That's one," I winked at my son. "Doesn't seem hard to me," I finished as I could see the light bulbs going off in his head. Kindness is the way! Kindness is king in this world, and collecting smiles reminds me of the game of Pac-Man. I want to start gobbling them up.

If you've been feeling stagnant or unfulfilled in your journey, maybe there's something in this mantra that can help. Start reaching out to others with a kind word, spreading kindness like frigging glitter or Frank's RedHot. Sprinkle that shit on *everything*. Kindness is the key. The more people you can be kind to, the more goodness you're going to get back. And before you know it, you're surrounded by a tribe of people who love you, who support you, who care about you.

Why? Because you sprinkled kindness first. You extended the olive branch. You don't know how many people in your life are suffering. They need a friend just like you. They are waiting for you to show up and be their friend, to be that light. And instead, we're all sitting in our little boxes, our little cubbies of solitude, not realizing that we are the masters of our lives.

Let's dig a little deeper now. Spreading kindness comes in two parts. You can't only sprinkle kindness out to everyone else. You have to sprinkle kindness to yourself, as well. Mind your thoughts, Booboo. Mind your thoughts. If your thoughts are negative, your actions are going to be negative, and if your actions are negative, no one's going to want to play with you on the playground anyway. Start here. You cannot win the battle outside until you can start winning the battle inside. We win with kindness.

Speak kindly to yourself when you're lying in bed at night, don't think, *oh my god, I'm so fat*. Instead, think, *I'm getting healthy. I'm capable of making healthier choices. I'm moving to a better space in my body.* These two thought processes are drastically different. One is kind, and one is not. So if you find yourself looking for something more positive and purposeful in your life, this might be a good place to begin.

Ugly thoughts embed themselves into your body in the form of tension. You can experience knots in your shoulders, kinks in your neck, flare-ups in your sciatica, and migraines. These symptoms could all be directly related to your thoughts and the people that you're surrounding yourself with. If you're with a bunch of crabs in the bucket and they're continually poking at you, telling you that you're not good enough, it's going to start manifesting itself into your physical body.

There is healing medicine in kindness. Your thoughts have so much power, not only in your mind but over your body. If you're not healthy, you might want to consider your thought processes.

Start speaking kindly to yourself and those around you. You will begin to reap abundance in the form of joy, in the form of connection, in the form of relationships that are supportive, healthy, and loving. Who does not want more of that in their life? Sign me up all day.

HOW MANY SMILES DID YOU COLLECT THIS WEEK?

MONDAY: _____

TUESDAY: _____

WEDNESDAY: _____

THURSDAY: _____

FRIDAY: _____

SATURDAY: _____

SUNDAY: _____

WHAT ARE SOME NEGATIVE THOUGHTS YOU WERE ABLE TO REDIRECT TO A KINDER NARRATIVE?

_____

_____

_____

_____

_____

_____

WEEK 46

LOOK AT MY FATHER

Story Time- In an effort to determine why some people overcome terrible adversity and others don't, a local university did a study. They wanted to figure out whether what made people survivors was genetic or some other factor? The best way to do that is to study a set of identical twin boys.

They followed the boys throughout their life. Now, these boys did not have a comfortable life. In fact, they had pretty hard experiences during their childhood. The mom worked all the time, picking up nights and weekend shifts to keep the lights on. The dad was an abusive alcoholic who struggled to keep a job because of his temper and addiction.

The boys suffered physical, mental, and verbal abuse at the hands of their raging father. It wasn't a very healthy environment for the children and both boys grew up with lasting scars. The study followed both boys into their mid-thirties.

The first son ended up falling in with the wrong crowd and dropping out of high school. He turned to alcohol and drugs to take away the pain resulting in several run-ins with the police and going to jail. Just like his father, he couldn't keep a job and found himself living off the government.

In contrast, the second son made dramatically different choices. He not only graduated high school but attended community college to get a degree. After college, he secured a high paying job, married his high school sweetheart, and bought a home. In the evenings, he could be found coaching his kid's athletic teams and volunteering at local shelters.

At the end of the study, the university arranged a final interview with both boys. "How did your life turn out this way?" they asked. The first son, who was an alcoholic and had been in and out of jail, said, "How could it not? Look at my father." When they interviewed the second son, they asked him the same question. "How did your life turn out this way?" To everyone's surprise, he said the same thing. "How could it not. Look at my father?"

One boy used his past as a reason to continue living a terrible life, to justify all of his poor choices. And one boy used it as fuel to improve his life, as an example of what he didn't want to be. One boy let his circumstances destroy him, and one boy let his circumstances define him.

I've been very transparent with you about my painful past, sharing how I came from the gutter. I always wondered why some people make it out, and some people don't. When I heard this story while I was in Utah recently, it struck me right in the heart.

The people who make it out, use their pain as fuel. I want you guys to think about all of the terrible things that have happened to you in your life. How are they playing in your story? You have a choice whether you let those things destroy you or define you.

These things are the notes of your victory song. They give you a testimony, prove you're a survivor and show the world you are a freaking warrior! Your trials were given to you for a reason. So many people right now are going through similar circumstances and are rolling over and dying because of it. They're giving up.

The difference is mindset. You are not broken. The storms and struggles of life cannot break you unless you let them. It's time to get a fire in your belly. Wake up with some passion and go out there and change your life for the better. We are cycle-breakers!

HOW HAVE YOU USED YOUR PAST AS AN EXCUSE?

_____

_____

_____

_____

_____

_____

WHAT DOES BEING A CYCLE BREAKER MEAN TO YOU AND HOW WILL IT IMPACT FUTURE GENERATIONS?

_____

_____

_____

_____

_____

_____

_____

_____

WEEK 47

TRANSFORMER OR TRANSMITTER

I have always hated running. For as long as I could remember, I have never been able to run for any considerable distance. I tried out for cross country running in the 8th grade because my friend was a runner on the team. I barely got off the school property before throwing in the towel and trying out for basketball instead.

When I joined the Army, my peers often struggled with the discipline and the yelling, the restricted freedom, or being disconnected from their families, but not me. That didn't bother me one bit. You know what I struggled with? All the damn running! I could sprint, but I couldn't run long distances. I almost didn't graduate basic training because of it.

I could not understand as a grown woman who could turn her body into a yogic pretzel, why this wasn't happening for me. I would rationalize it with statements like, "I am not built like that" or "I don't know how people do it." Then I would surround myself with other people who despised running as much as I did to make myself feel validated.

It wasn't until I challenged myself to figure out what was broken in my head to make me stop every single time. As I worked on unpacking my baggage around my inability to run, a memory from my childhood came back to me. My abusive stepfather used to make us run as punishment. He would keep us outside in the dead of winter for hours just running, back and forth, across this big field that backed up to our trailer. We would be forced to run in the mornings before the sun came up and at night in the dark. I remember knowing that stopping would end in a "whooping," so I never stopped.

Running was a trigger, now I could see it more clearly. I found a huge roadblock in my brain from the trauma of all those bad running experiences. I cried hard that day. I'm talking ugly cried. I was 37 years old and I was still finding these deep seeds of pain that he planted in me.

What happens when you hold that kind of pain inside of you? You don't release the pressure that's building inside. It keeps growing bigger and bigger because you won't face it, because you won't go through the process of healing from it. Sometimes it's not our fault. I had blocked out those memories for so long I didn't even realize I was holding onto the pain.

Not only will it keep building up, but eventually, it is going to start bubbling over. You become snappy with your husband, impatient with your children, and irritated with your friends. You don't want to be this way, but it just comes out. You are officially transmitting your pain to those around you, like an STD. There is an actual medical term for it called displaced aggression.

There's a common saying that you may have heard, "hurt people hurt." Newsflash everybody has been hurt and experienced some suffering. I don't know a single person who hasn't been through something traumatic and painful in their lives. It's not an excuse to be a dirk.

Their pain is showing. They are hurting and taking it out on the ones they love. The only way to stop doing this is by doing the hard work. You have to look in the mirror and have the courage to sit in your pain. That is the key. Once we can identify our grief, we release a pressure valve inside our hearts and can then begin the process of transforming the emotions.

Once I had clarity around my distaste of running, I started using that memory as fuel to say, Screw You Stepdad! I can do this and you're not going to stop me from transforming my life. A switch flipped inside me and I just started running, 20-30 minutes without stopping. This was a huge breakthrough. I didn't build up to it or train using one of those couch to 5k apps. I did that harder work of unpacking my shit and found myself free. I converted my pain of my trauma into fuel versus using it as a crutch.

If you know someone negative, a Debbie Downer that snaps back at people for no reason, I would suggest gifting them this book and extending a mountain of compassion their way. The jabs that they take out on you are nothing compared to the storm that's raging inside their heads. Become acutely aware of when you're edges are frayed when you find yourself saying things out of character and ask yourself where they could be coming from.

We collectively as a human race are not going to get better until we're willing to start looking at our pain and embracing it as a tool to get to something better. This week we commit to stop letting it spill out and negatively impacting those around us because I know that's not what you want. I know you don't want to hurt the people around you. Transform your pain instead. Convert it into fuel and go out there and start becoming the person that you want to be.

DID YOU UNINTENTIONALLY SNAP
AT ANYONE THIS WEEK OR RECENTLY?

_____

_____

_____

_____

_____

_____

WERE THERE OTHER THINGS ON YOUR MIND
THAT MADE YOU TESTIER?

_____

_____

_____

_____

_____

_____

WEEK 48

FOLLOW THE ENVY

Have you heard the saying, we don't see the world as it is, but we see the world as we are? This little powerhouse nugget is something I always try to keep in mind when others share their opinions with me. We have these ideas of what the world is like based on our experiences, our education levels, our socioeconomic classes, and how our parents brought us up. Everyone has a way that they see the world, a perspective that is different from anyone else's.

I've wanted to write a book for years but always discounted myself as unworthy. The idea would pop into my heart and I would dismiss it. "I'm not a scholar," I would think to myself. But here's the thing, we each have a valuable perspective. It's a small puzzle piece to a larger picture. The courage arrived to write this book when I paired the quote above with this weeks' mantra.

I've had a couple of people in my life write books, including my brother. Envy stirred every time I heard about someone else, doing something I secretly wanted to do. This nagging feeling would not go away, and so

I knew I had to try.

This week I wanted to talk about this concept of following your envy. Envy gets a bad rap. I think it has been stigmatized to be this evil thing that we want to avoid and pretend that doesn't exist. But I believe, based on my personal experience, that envy is very real, and I think everyone experiences it.

To that point, it's not this bad monster that we should all be trying to avoid. There are parts of envy that can turn negative, but the actual sensation that you feel when you see someone with something that you want is not a bad thing. It's a bread crumb to your destiny. We are all born, not knowing what we want to do in this world. Every time your envy is triggered, it's a sign to your spirit that it's something that you want in your life.

What makes it harmful is that instead of happiness for others, we wish ill upon them. Resentment festers. We tap into our scarcity mindset and think that there's not enough for us. Then it turns into jealousy and anger. This week I want to flip the script on envy.

What if instead of avoidance, we honed our Spidey senses and become acutely aware of it. Envy becomes a tool to guide you towards the things you want in your life. Other people having them is only reinforcing that you can obtain it too.

Stop thinking that somebody else having something means that there's less for you. Maybe they were put in your path to be a lighthouse of proof that it's possible. Connecting to your envy is a chance for you to start to learn about yourself and what your dreams and desires are. The universe will never give you something you hate, so use the envy to bless that which you desire.

If you see a girl who looks banging in her dress and you're carrying around an extra 20 pounds, instead of throwing some side-eye at her redirect your thoughts. That girl looks amazing, and I can't wait until I experience that same thing.

Pro-tip: if you really want to level up, tell her she looks good!

Bless that which you desire. You cannot receive things that you are throwing shade at and judging others for having. When you see someone, who has something that you want, recognize, celebrate, and vibrate higher. Be brave. Reach out to that person and say, "Do you have any advice for me? I want to create a business like that. Do you have any tips for me? I want to lose weight. How did you write your book? I want to write a book someday."

Envy becomes terrible when it turns into jealousy, cattiness, and throwing shade. There is a trend lately to "serve tea," which is basically a pass to rip people apart and gossip about them, under the guise of keeping it real, or just being honest. Pay close attention to how often you are serving tea because you are indirectly blocking your blessings.

When you see someone carrying the torch, something that you want to manifest in your life, it is your responsibility to chase it!

WHO DID YOU CHEER FOR THIS WEEK?

_____

_____

_____

_____

_____

WHAT IS SOMETHING YOU HAVE ALWAYS WANTED TO DO BUT HAVEN'T?

_____

_____

_____

_____

_____

_____

_____

DO YOU KNOW ANYONE WHO HAS ACCOMPLISHED THIS, AND CAN YOU REACH OUT?

WEEK 49

ARE YOU THE COW OR THE PIG?

Story Time- This one is quick, but it packs a punch and is one of my favorite stories. It's called The Cow and the Pig.

The Cow and the Pig are enjoying a summer day on the farm. After some time, the Pig has a serious question for the Cow. He says, "Cow, why does everybody love you more than me?"

"I don't even get it." continues the Pig. "You only give them milk every day. I don't understand why they love you, and they loathe me. I give them bacon for their breakfast, and ham for their holidays. They make brushes with my bristles and some of them even pickle my feet." the Pig is starting to get upset. "I give them so much, and they love you more than me, even though all you do is give them milk."

The Cow thinks about it for a moment, and then he says, "maybe it's because I give while I'm still alive."

That's such a compelling point. How many of us are sitting on our gifts?

Waiting for the "right time?" Planning for when the conditions are perfect, and for circumstances to align? Some of you right now are even waiting for permission. That never happens, so we end up just waiting our whole life.

How sad would it be to get to the end of your life and realize you had a well of talent that you never even used? You had all of these gifts, and you just let them sit. You just waited and waited until it was too late, and you wasted it.

This week I challenge you to give generously in your life, not just with your money, but with your time *and* with your talent. Use those gifts that you have inside of you. Do not wait one more minute to start harvesting and giving to the world.

I wanted to write a book for years and never did. What changed? I decided to stop waiting for conditions to be perfect. It's like having a baby. You can read all the books and take the Lamaze classes to prepare as much as possible. But when the time comes, you could still feel scared and unprepared. We are *never* going to be prepared for give birth to our dreams.

It may also hurt a bit, not going to lie. This book has challenged me to push myself harder than I ever have before. I've cried, been frustrated, and worried about doing it right many times. Not doing it, though, would hurt a lot more. Knowing I was wasting my chance to do something I've always wanted to do.

What you have inside of you is unique. I want you to find the courage to use it. To realize that you've got these beautiful gifts and to start living more fully. Generosity is an abundance lifestyle. It's about giving just as much as you want to receive.

Money, yes, but also your time, your emotions, and your talents too.

You become alive by giving all of the fantastic stuff that you have inside of you. Stop waiting. Stop living in fear that people are going to reject you.

I'm not special. All I am is courageous enough to get out there and say, "You know what? I'm done with the monotonous life. I'm not going to continue wasting it. I'm ready for more, and I'm willing to ask for abundance." We are done waiting!

LIST 3 OF YOUR TALENTS:

_____

_____

_____

_____

_____

_____

HOW CAN YOU SHARE THEM MORE?

_____

_____

_____

_____

_____

_____

WEEK 50

STOP MILKING IT

I had a fascinating conversation with my son last night. He is 11 years old, and he was gifted tickets for him and his entire football team to go to the Ravens football game. My husband and I couldn't take him because we both had work obligations, but he was fortunate enough to have one of the other parents offer to give him a ride and to watch him through the entire game to make sure he wasn't kidnapped.

He had an amazing day at the game. We went on a walk, and he's telling me about it. He starts off sharing with me how fun it was; he showed me the souvenirs he bought. After a few minutes, he starts talking about the parking situation. He's going through all the inconveniences, complaining about the end of the game, and having to sit in traffic. Leaving the game was a nightmare. It took them an hour plus to get out of the parking garage and to get home. The parking attendants didn't know what they were doing, and the garage was poorly designed, he told me. And don't even get him started on how expensive it was to park, $40 is robbery. We have now been talking about the parking garage longer than any of the fun stuff that happened.

I had to stop him at this point, "Babe, this was only one hour of your whole day. There were 23 good hours that you seem to be forgetting about and you're spending all of this time, all of this energy focused on the one bad hour. That doesn't seem right." He thinks for a moment and says, "Yea, well, I was sleeping for 8 of those hours, so they don't count." Moments like this make me question all my parenting choices.

I looked at him and said, "Honey, you are fortunate enough to live in a house where you can sleep safely for eight hours. We live in a lovely home, and you have your room and a bed with blankets. You have heat and air conditioning and not to mention parents who protect you while you sleep."

Be very mindful of spinning your wheels. Start to notice when you're moanin and groanin about life. It has become prevalent to victimize ourselves by complaining, sometimes making it a competition of who's day was worse. We've glorified being disaffected. Spend a few minutes on any social media platform, and you will see what I mean. There are entire Reddit threads dedicated to tearing people down and complaining about the injustices with no intent of finding a solution. Complaining for complaining's sake.

But be cautious of that slippery slope, because you will trick yourself into believing that you don't have a good life, that you do not have things that you need often provided to you. You are going to become blind to your blessings. Your life is an echo chamber. What you say, what you put out is going to keep circulating around and around and around until you've convinced yourself that you've got the crappiest life on the planet, even after you've had the best day ever.

I read a meme one time that said: Was it a bad day, or a bad five minutes you milked all day?

I am not saying that you shouldn't voice your concerns in situations when it is necessary but ask yourself these questions to determine whether or not it's worth your time.

- Can I change the situation?
- Is it causing me or others harm?
- Are my words adding insight or value?
- Is it any of my business?
- Will it matter a year from now?

If you answered "no" to one or more of those questions, tread lightly. These pitfalls are just distractions from the goodness in your life.

WERE THERE ANY TIMES THIS WEEK WHEN ONE BAD INCIDENT TURNED INTO A BAD DAY?

_____

_____

_____

_____

_____

WHAT CAN YOU DO NEXT TIME TO PREVENT THE SPIRAL?

_____

_____

_____

_____

_____

WEEK 51

WHO HOLDS THE KEYS?

Grab your pen- before we get into this week's mantra, I want to ask you a question.

How do you define abundance? _____

_____

_____

_____

It's a big word, and it has a lot of meaning for different people. For the longest time, I thought abundance meant mansions and millionaires. It was champagne wishes and caviar dreams. I thought it meant surplus. But this week, I'd like to re-examine with you guys what abundance actually means.

I no longer think that abundance implies excess. Now that I've gotten older and wiser, I believe abundance means having precisely what you need when you need it. You don't have more, and you don't have less. More than what you need would be wasteful.

This past weekend I drove up to New York because I was asked to speak at a training. It was an o'dark thirty wake-up call. Followed by four and a half hours commute there and another four and a half hours back, and sandwiched in between was six hours of training where I had to speak. I know I've mentioned my social anxiety before, and it always flares when I'm asked to speak. I get all wrapped up. Being a public speaker does not come naturally to me. So it's not only stressful but draining.

I didn't get back home until eleven o'clock that night. I had to decompress because my brain was wired. I laid in bed until almost 1 o'clock in the morning before finally falling asleep. When my alarm went off at 6:30 the next morning, I felt a sharp pain in my heart.

I have to physically force my body out of bed to teach my early morning yoga class. A quick pit-stop in the bathroom to brush my teeth and slap on deodorant, and I'm out the door. Okay, you guys real talk, I am *not* a morning person. I need coffee to help me form proper sentences.

Finally, I pulled into Dunkin Donuts, and I made my order. I drive up to the window and guess who forgot their wallet?!?! Are you effing kidding me! I was on the brink of a stage 4 nuclear meltdown. Tired and drained were terrible, but now I have to deal with the shame of not having money. News flash: being broke is a big trigger for me.

My face flushed as I pulled up to the window bracing myself for the pathetic look the drive-thru attendant was going to give me. "I'm so sorry." I eeked out. "I forgot my wallet," and I was getting ready to pull away, empty-handed.

Do you believe in angels? On this day I met one. The kind soul working the window says to me, "No worries, ma'am, you're one of our regulars. I see you all the time. Go ahead and take it. Just pay me for it next time."

Now, if I wasn't going to cry before, I'm crying now, because that is literally what abundance is. Abundance is getting exactly what you need when you need it. I am not even mad that he called me "ma'am."

But there's a kicker to this week's nugget. You never know who's holding the keys to your next blessing. I was already prejudging this saint before I even knew who it was. I assumed he would think I was a liar just trying to get a free meal, the same way I had judged panhandlers on the street corners.

We are so closed off in our society, and we don't even make eye contact with people walking down the street. We walk by hundreds of people daily and keep our nose in our phone as a shield. What if one of those people has the key to your next blessing? They could change your day or even your life, but we aren't open to them. As a result, the blessing passes us by.

We think that our blessings have to come in "this shape" and "this size" on "this day" at "this time." We build a wall around ourselves and only let in the things that line up with our preconceived ideas. That wall might keep out stuff you don't want, but it is also keeping out the good things that are trying to get to you.

At that moment, in the Dunkin Donuts drive-thru, I needed a coffee more than I needed a million dollars, and the universe provided. It wasn't exactly the way I thought I would get it (i.e. being a paying customer), but I received precisely what I needed when I needed it.

CAN YOU REMEMBER A TIME WHEN SOMETHING
SHOWED UP JUST WHEN YOU NEEDED IT?

_____

_____

_____

_____

_____

_____

HOW WERE YOU OPEN THIS WEEK TO THE PEOPLE AROUND YOU?

_____

_____

_____

_____

_____

_____

_____

WEEK 52

TIME TO ROAR

Story Time- A pregnant tiger was hunting in a large open field when she came across a heard of goats. She pounced on the herd but because she was full term, she wasn't fast enough, and the herd scattered. The aggressive hunt sent the momma tiger into labor on the field, and due to some complications, the mother died after giving birth.

The newborn cub was left defenseless in the wild. After a few hours passed, the goat herd returned to the feeding ground. They discovered the cub and decided to take the baby in and raise him. They protected him from the elements, taught him to eat grass and bleat like the rest of the herd.

A few months passed before an older male tiger came along and discovered the cub with the goats. "What are you doing with these goats, young one?" he asked. "Baaaaaa" said the cub. "Really?" pressed the larger tiger. "This is my family," replied the cub. "But you are a tiger, and tigers don't hang out with goats." The big tiger scoffed. "I am a goat!" exclaimed the cub. "No, you are a tiger, come with me, and I will prove it to you." The older tiger demanded.

They traveled together into the jungle until they came to a clearing in the trees, which gave way to a fishing pond. The water was calm on this bright summer day. "Look in the water and tell me what you see," the older tiger barked. So, the cub hesitantly peeked over the edge.

The cub double blinked, turning his head right and left in confusion. This is not at all what he thought he would see. He doesn't look anything like his family, and this is very alarming to the cub. "Follow me," the older tiger said as he walked off towards the tree line.

After a trek up the mountainside, the older tiger brings the young cub into his den, where he has a freshly killed antelope. "Here, eat this," he told the cub. The cub was mortified, "I am a vegetarian," he proclaims, but the older tiger is not having any of that nonsense. "Eat!" he says firmly.

The cub takes a bite. "Not bad," he thinks and takes another bite. Something starts to happen, the cub has never felt so hungry, and he digs in. He feels a rush of energy from the food, and his chronic belly ache has gone away.

Suddenly, the older tiger hits the young cub. Stunned, the baby tiger takes a step back. The older tiger takes another swipe at him, "Stop" whines the cub, but the bigger tiger keeps on swatting him, left and then right paw. The young tiger backs into the corner, looking for a place to hide. The older tiger has the young cub backed into a corner and starts beating him down.

The young cub starts out whining, but then there's a shift, he feels something else bubbling up inside; with each hit from the other tiger, it gets stronger and stronger. The young cub is angry now and cannot take one more hit. The bubbling in his belly builds up until he can't contain it anymore and he lets out a roar!

This story always gives me all the goosies. I think we can all relate to this story on some level, but what stands out to me is how often we assimilate to fit in. Sometimes, like the cub, we do it for survival. Other times, we do it for fear of judgment or rejection.

Humans also have herd tendencies. We have this deep-seeded desire to fit in and be a part of the community. We need the connection to survive, but at what cost are we getting it? Who are we pretending to be, and how is it helping us?

Throughout our lives, our family and friends have shaped our reality. They taught us who to be and how to act to fit in. The underlying problem is that there are gifts inside you now lying dormant. Sometimes they ask us to temper our talents because of their insecurities and sometimes it's because they don't know any better.

It's when we surround ourselves with other tigers that we can see ourselves more clearly. When we starting feeding our souls with the knowledge the nourishes us, we get stronger. Unfortunately, sometimes it takes getting knocked around by life a little to find your voice.

This week, our last week together, I want you to roar! You have been doing the work, growing your confidence, and finding your courage. Now it is time to step into who you were called to be.

IN WHAT WAYS HAVE YOU BEEN PLAYING SMALL?

_____

_____

_____

_____

_____

_____

HOW DO YOU WANT TO ROAR
IN THE YEAR TO COME?

_____

_____

_____

_____

_____

_____

FINAL THOUGHTS

Wow, it is hard to believe this book is coming to an end. I know some weeks challenged you. Some of them may have made you uncomfortable and asked you to look at your life differently. I'm sure some weeks inspired you and created space for you to change your life. I am proud of you for not giving up and doing the work.

To reflect on what you have accomplished, I want to go back to the beginning. Before we end, we need to look at how far we've come. It's time to go back and read that letter you wrote to yourself at the start of our journey. Go ahead; I will wait.

How does it feel looking back?

What do you wish you could tell that version of yourself?

Were there any things you learned about yourself that you didn't expect?

How do you feel about the next chapter of your life?

I wrote this book intending to help you understand yourself better. You have transformed it into a living and breathing reflection of your growth. Each book was printed with the same content, but as you hold it in your hands now, I hope you realize that we created something special together, something unique. Flip through these pages, notice your journey. Do the things you wrote still hold true? Which mantra touched your heart the most?

I want to know! If you have made it this far and haven't joined our online community, you should consider doing that now. We have been waiting for you. You don't have to stop growing if you don't want to. Gather with us as we link arms and support each other. There is a seat for you at the table, and I cannot wait to connect with you. Until then I will always be here with you in the pages of this book. Namaste my friends.